THE
PRATAPGAD WAR
RISE OF THE HINDU BADSHAH
CHHATRAPATI SHIVAJI MAHARAJ

DR. HEMANTRAJE GAIKWAD

BLUEROSE PUBLISHERS
India | U.K.

Copyright © Dr. Hemantraje Gaikwad 2024

All rights reserved by author. No part of this publication may be reproduced, stored in a retrieval system or transmitted in any form or by any means, electronic, mechanical, photocopying, recording or otherwise, without the prior permission of the author. Although every precaution has been taken to verify the accuracy of the information contained herein, the publisher assumes no responsibility for any errors or omissions. No liability is assumed for damages that may result from the use of information contained within.

BlueRose Publishers takes no responsibility for any damages, losses, or liabilities that may arise from the use or misuse of the information, products, or services provided in this publication.

For permissions requests or inquiries regarding this publication, please contact:

BLUEROSE PUBLISHERS
www.BlueRoseONE.com
info@bluerosepublishers.com
+91 8882 898 898
+4407342408967

ISBN: 978-93-6452-933-4

Cover design: Shivam
Typesetting: Namrata Saini

First Edition: September 2024

Dedication

This book is dedicated to my life long friends
Dr Maitri and Shri Yogesh Gupta.

In Gratitude

Vijayrao Deshmukh

Gajanan B. Mehendale

Babasaheb Purandare

P. K. Ghanekar

Capt Ganesh Modak

Kindly Note

1- The word caste is used in the medieval context and it has no significance now.

2- Before his coronation Shivaji Raje is addressed as Raje and only after his coronation is he addressed as Chhatrapati Maharaj.

3- All maps are not to scale. An attempt has been made to draw maps so that the reader may understand sites and distances.

4- The same person or place may be spelled differently as per the reference from where they were quoted.

Preface

At the very outset let me be frank in admitting that I am an Ophthalmic Surgeon and have no training in the study of History. However, my first book "Shivaji Maharaj The Greatest" has been published in English, Marathi and Hindi. It compares Shivaji Maharaj with other great medieval warriors like Alexander, Caeser, Hannibal, Attila, Ghenghis Khan, Richard the Great, William Wallace, Gastavus and Napoleon. I had also compared him with two Indian warriors namely Akbar and Aurangzeb.

I am very happy to announce that based on this book a documentary has been produced in Hindi, Marathi and English. I am hopeful that very soon both the book and the documentary will be available in Kannada, Bangla and Sanskrit besides other languages.

The present book 'The Pratapgad War' discusses the importance of the period from April 1659 to 06 April 1663, wherein Shivaji Raje strikes three stunning blows ie the elimination of Afzal Khan, the escape from Panhalgad, and the strike into Shaista Khan's camp. These three incidents catapulted him from a upstart rebel son of a Bijapuri Jagirdar's son to a Hindu Badshah.

I am most grateful to Ms Yukta Gothankar my enthusiastic assistant for overseeing everything that went into writing this book. Her greatest achievement was to develop a new way of drawing informative maps. The book is made up of 200 pages and has more than 20 maps.

Next, I wish to thank my other staff members of Dr Gaikwad Institute who managed the Institute while I concentrated on the book. They are Bhakti Parab, Swati Surve, Pranali Shelar and Purva Gaikwad.

Along with my staff members, many of my students typed the hundreds and hundreds of pages that went into the making of the basic manuscript of this book. They are Aditi Mulik, Mansi Pawar, Rohanta Salvi, Sakshi Matkar, Pranali Khondage and Namita Gaikwad.

I am grateful to Shri Saurabh Lohogaonkar for his guidance in translating the 'Adnyandas cha Powada.'

I am also grateful to Shri Ranjan Gawde for allowing me to use the photographs for the cover.

I wish to thank my publishers – the BlueRose Publishers, especially Ankita who took a personal interest in the making of this book.

And of course I must not forget my family, wife Dr Pushpa, son Dr Gaurang, daughter Dr Gunjan, son in law Harshal and grandson Hruday all of whom make life worth living.

Dr Hemant Raje Gaikwad

Conversion Tables

1 League = 4.8 km

1 Mound = 37.8 kg

20 Mound = 1 Khandi

= 750 kg

1 s(h)er ie seer = 1 litre

1 Ton = 1000 kg

1 Hon = 2.7 to 3 gm

1 Nautical Mile =

1 Kos = 4000 Yard = 2.5 m = 4.0 km

1111 Shake +78 =1189 Gregorian date

1111 A Hijri + 690 = 1701 Gregorian date

1 Tola = 116 gm

Rate of Gold Rs. 10 = 11.66 grams (tola) gold

An infantry soldier was paid Rs three

A cavalry man was paid Rs ten

Average wage was Rs two/three per month

One ghadi was equivalent to 24 minutes.

Choghadiya was equivalent to 96 minutes.

One pal was equivalent to 24 seconds.

2.5 ghadi was equivalent to 60 minutes ie 1 hour.

2.5 pal was equivalent to 60 seconds ie 1 minute.

Contents

CHAPTER ONE 1
    The Deccan. 1
    Maharashtra. 1
    Hindus in Muslim Adilshahi. 4
    Shahaji Bhosle 1622 -1654. 5
    Shahaji's jagir in Pune. 7
    Gadhwa Cha Nangar. 10
    Jijamata's Sonyacha Nangar. (Golden Plow) 11
    Social Engineering by Shivaji Raje. 12
    Watandars and Jahgirdars. 13
    The Oath at Rohireshwar 1642-1645. 14
    The seal of Shivaji Maharaj. 15
    The Early Days. 17
    Aurangzeb's Invasion Of Bijapur 19
    Battle Of Kalyani-Bidar. 20
    Mughal war of Succession 21
    Shahaji disowns Shivaji Raje. 22

CHAPTER TWO 24
    Jawli 1656. 24
    The campaign against the Mores 26
    More Objects To Shivaji Raje. 27
    Tulja Bhawani 30
    Shivaji Raje's status after Jawli 31
    Passes of Jawli 32
    Aurangzeb warns about Shivaji Raje 33
    Aurangzeb advices Adilshah on Shiva(ji). 36
    Shahaji Bhosle and his eldest son Sambhaji. 36

Arrest of Shahaji 38
Battle of Purandar (1648-49) 39
Standard /Flags 40
Shivaji Raje corresponds with Shehzada Murad Baksh 41
Shahaji Raje released 43

CHAPTER THREE 45

Why Adilshahi decided to attack Shivaji Raje? 45
Who was Afzal Khan 46
Ali Adilshah Appoints Afzal Khan 47
Afzal Khan was a successful general 50
Afzal Khan was a ruthless administrater. 50
The War Scenario 1659 52
A MUGHAL -MARATHA COMBINATION 52
Afzal Khan 's harem 53
Cenotaph of Afzal Khan 56
Departure from Bijapur (April 1659) 56
Afzal Khan's Army 56
The Preparations by Afzal Khan. 58
Omens 59
Afzal Khan's Strategy 59
Afzal Khan's Tortuous Route 60
The Bajaji Nimbalkar Episode 60
This was the second turning point of the Pratapgad battle. 61
SWOT Analysis by Shivaji Raje 62
"Time for Space." 62
Afzal Khan makes Wai his base. 63
The situation in June 1659. 63
Kanhoji Jedhe 64
This was the third turning point in the Battle of Pratapgad. 64

CHAPTER FOUR 66

Shivaji Raje's strategic retreat to Jawli. 66

Afzal Khan wins the fist round.. 67
'Defence in Depth' Strategy of Shivaji Raje......................... 68
Morale of Afzal Khan 's Troops 69
Morale of Shivaji Raje's troops. 69
Role of climate and terrain in war.. 71
The Reasons for Negotiations... 73
Shivaji Raje 's spies.. 74
Afzal Khan sent the Envoy first. 75
Shivaji Raje sent Pantaji Gopinath as his envoy. 75
Afzal Khan 's envoy Krishnaji Bhaskar................................ 76
This was the Sixth turning point in the Pratapgad battle. 79
Why did Afzal Khan decide on a meeting? 79
Afzal's willingness to come to Pratapgad was the seventh turning point. 82
Greedy Traders.. 82
The Mughal system of hunting animals............................... 83
The Protocol for the Meet 85
Netoji Palkar 87
Afzal Khan's Camp... 87
Afzal Khan marches to Jawli 88
Afzal Khan reaches Jawli... 90
Morale of the Maratha camp 1-9 November........................ 90

CHAPTER FIVE 92

Shivaji Raje' s strategy prior to the meet- November 7,8,9. .. 92
The death of Shivaji Raje's elder brother Sambhaji.............. 92
The morale of the troops of Afzal Khan on 7,8,9 November 94
Readying for the encounter. 96
Time frame of the visits of Shivaji Raje, Pantaji, Krishnaji and Afzal Khan 96
Eight possible options at the meeting. 97
In case of option -6, if Shivaji Raje was imprisoned. 99
In case of option – 7, if there was a treaty............................. 99

In case of option -8, Afzal Khan could die but the Bijapur army could take Pratapgad Fort. 100
10 November 1659 : 6.00 AM to 1.00 PM 101
Afzal Khan :1.00 PM to 1.30 PM. 102
Shivaji Raje: 1.00 PM to 1.30 PM. 103
The Shivaji Raje -Afzal Khan Meeting :
2.00 PM to 2.15 PM 106
The Embrace : 2.15 PM to 3.00 PM. 107
Was there a treachery? Who used the weapon first? 109
Trumpets at 3.00 PM. 110
Krishna Bhaskar. 111
Cannons fired at 3.15 PM. 112

CHAPTER SIX 114

The Battle of Koyana. 114
Netoji's Attack on Wai. 116
Destruction of Afzal Khan's Army. 116
After the Battle. 117
Mannuchi 118
Exploitation of the victory :15 Forts in 17 days 121
Netoji's March. 122
The Marathas descended into the Konkan (November 1659- January 1660). 122

CHAPTER SEVEN 124

Battle of Kolhapur. 124
Shaista Khan's Mughal Army Invade Deccan 125
Marathas attack suburbs of Bijapur -Mid April 1660 128
Siddi Jauhar - the Lion of Kurnool. 129
Siddi Johar traps Shivaji Raje in Panhala. 131
2 April to 5 June 1660 -The Revington Affair. 133
Battle Of Chakan June-Aug 1661. 134
Shivaji Raje makes a daring plan. 136
Maharaj Escapes from Panhala (13 July 1660). 137

The Bandals and the Battle of Ghod Khind 138
 Battle Of Umberkhind 1661. (Map 7/8) 141
 Lightening strike on Shaista Khan at Lal Mahal. 145

CHAPTER EIGHT 148

 Analysis of The Pratapgad War 148
 a- Shivaji Raje and San Zu 148
 b-Wagh nakh, what and why? 149
 c- Shivaji Raje and World History. 150
 d-Role of Shiva Kashid at siege of Panhalgad.................... 151
 e-Role of Shivaji Raje and geography. 152
 f- Afzal Khan's galbat and the Maratha Navy. 153
 Spies 153
 Shivaji Maharaj and Astronomy 154
 Legacy of Shivaji Raje 160
 1680 to 1707 160
 After Aurangzeb's death (1707 to 1759) 160

CHAPTER NINE 164

 Epilogue... 164

CHAPTER TEN.. 167

 Wagh Nakh presented to James Grant Duff...................... 175
 Danpatta : State Weapon of Maharashtra.......................... 177
 Appendix 182
 Adnyandas cha Powada (Ballad) 182

CHRONOLOGY... 205

Dr Hemant Raje Gaikwad 211

CHAPTER ONE

The Deccan.

The Deccan plateau is mainly between 300 to 750 meters above sea level, and its general slope descends toward the east.

The Western Ghats, also called the Sahyadri, are a north-south chain of mountains or hills that mark the western edge of the Deccan plateau region. They rise abruptly from the coastal plain of the Arabian Sea as an escarpment of variable height, but their eastern slopes are much gentler. The Western Ghats contain a series of residual plateaus and peaks separated by saddles and passes. Some of the ghats are Bhor ghat, Pimpri ghat, Nane ghat, Amboli ghat, Bhimashankar ghat, Warghya ghat, Ambaghat, Bhopya ghat Shivlya ghat etc. Mahabaleshwar is the highest elevations in the northern half, rising to 1,430 meters. The Western Ghats receive heavy rainfall, and several major rivers—most notably the Krishna (Kistna) and the two holy rivers, the Godavari and the Kaveri (Cauvery)—have their headwaters there.

The Deccan is arid and hilly, a triangular plateau that rises from central India toward its southern tip, flanked by two mountain ranges, the Western and Eastern Ghats along its long coastlines: coasts which connected and influenced by Persia and Central Asia, to Greco-Roman and Southeast Asian trade.

As a result, the Deccan has been less agricultural, and more trade-oriented

Maharashtra.

The name Maharashtra was first mentioned in the seventh century by a Chinese traveller Huan Tsang. Four centuries ago, the name Maharashtra meant the western edge of the Deccan plateau i.e.

tract bounded on the north by Tapti river, on the south by the Krishna. It included the districts of Nasik, Pune, Satara, Ahmednagar and Solapur. It also included a tract between the Western Ghats and the Indian ocean called the Konkan.

Maharashtra was a barren rocky land compared to the lush green plains of the north. The rainfall is very low and uncertain, the cultivation is poor and precarious, the staple crops being bajra, jowar and ragi.

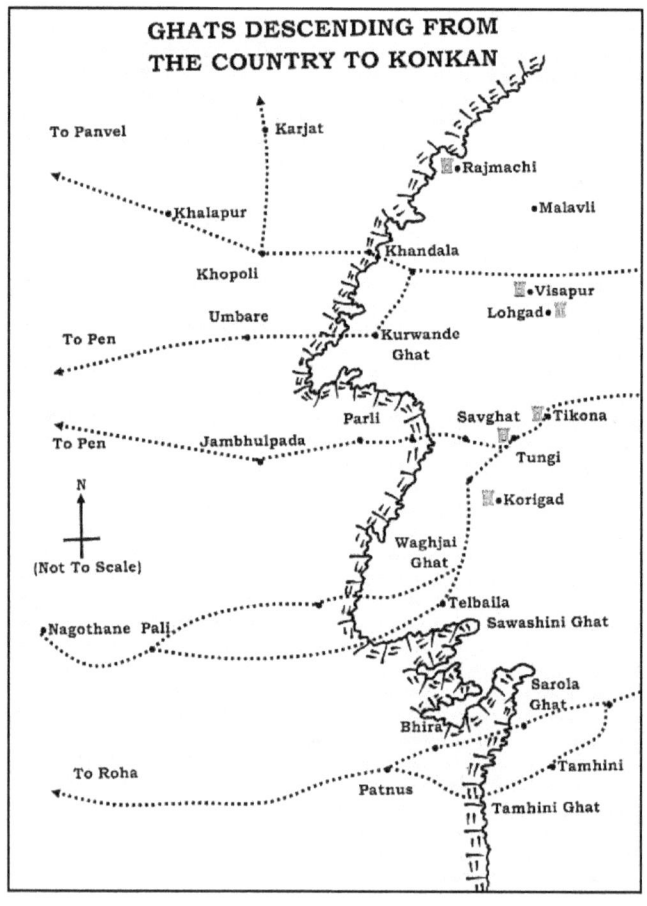

Fig 1/1

The whole of the Ghats and neighboring mountains often terminate towards the top of the in a wall of smooth rock, the highest points form natural fortresses. Traversing the ghats were many passes (1/1) where toll used to be collected. All the goods that came by sea at the ports of Bankot, Dabhol, Jaigad, Ratnagiri, Devgad, Malvan and Vengurla had to cross these ghats to go to the cities of Ahmednagar, Satara and Kolhapur, Bijapur and beyond.

As we shall see later the income from these tolls had made the Mores rich, arrogant and pompous.

The Deccan Sultanates .

The Deccan sultanates (MAP 1/2) were formed by the break-up of the Bahmani Sultanate. In 1490, Ahmadnagar, Bijapur and Berar gained independence, Golconda became independent in 1518, and Bidar in 1528.

THE FIVE DECCAN SULTANATES

Fig 1-2

The five sultanates were of diverse origin: the Ahmadnagar Sultanate was Brahmin-Hindu; the Berar Sultanate was Kanarese-Hindu; the Bidar Sultanate was founded by a former Turkic slave; the Bijapur Sultanate was founded by a Georgian-Oghuz Turkic slave; and the Golconda Sultanate was of Turkmen origin.

Hindus in Muslim Adilshahi.

Some of the regulations issued during Muhammad Adilshah's reign (1626 — 1656), were

(1) Only Muslims should be appointed as Governors to the provinces. Hindus could aspire only for clerical posts. They were debarred from executive posts, as they were disturbers of the land and the faith.

(2) As per the rules of Islam, no infidel could claim equality with a Muslim. If a Muslim happens to injure an infidel, he should only be admonished orally but never should he be punished.

(3) The Muslims should refrain from joining infidel celebrations like Holi, Diwali and Dashera. But they should not object or obstruct them.

Shivaji Raje was aghast to note that, his father Shahaji who had shown exemplary courage in the fight against the Mughals, for which he was given the jagir of Poona District and Banglore by the Adilshah and he was called Farzand (son), yet a suspicion that he failed in his duties, brought forth from the Adilshah a severe punishment. On 22 June 1644 the hand of his vakil was cut off. He was treated as a rebel and on 1 August 1644 orders were issued to seize his possessions in the Poona jagir.

The Bhosle family had a huge role to play in the Deccan.

Shahaji son of Maloji was born in 1599.

The Shivbharat 42-44 states that in 1613 he was married to Jijabai daughter of Lakhoji Jadhav.

Shahaji Bhosle 1622 -1654.

Fig 1-3 Shahaji Raje

The Shivbharat Ch4/ 30-47 states that in about 1615, the Nizamshah conveyed a Darbar at Daulatabad. Along with other sardars there were three families - the Jadhav family, the Bhosle family and the Khandagale family. The Jadhav family was related to the Bhosle family by marriage. i.e Jadhavrao's daughter Jijabai was married to Shahaji Bhosle the son of Maloji Bhosle. After the Darbar had dispersed for the day, the three families along with the other sardars came out. Suddenly, an elephant belonging to the Khandagale family went beserk and trampled to death some members of the Jadhav family. Enraged at the death of his family members Lakhoji Jadhav's son Dattaji attacked the Khandagales sword in hand. Seeing him in this belligerent state Shahaji Bhosle and his cousin Kheloji went to the defence of the Khandagales. So instead of everyone trying to control a raging elephant, what erupted was a full flegged skirmish where family and friends were at each other's throats. Things really got horrible when Shahaji killed his brother-in-law Dattaji Jadhav. This should have brought everybody to their senses but that did not happen, for a furious

Lakhoji attacked his son-in-law Shahaji and injured him on his arm so seriously that he fell down unconscious Fortunately by then the Nizam came to know of this madness and he sternly intervened putting a stop to this senseless and wanton killing.

The above episode clearly spells out the mentality of the Marathas. A slight affront even by mistake could make two related families draw daggers at each other. They would thirst for revenge for generation and what is more take great pride in it.

In 1622 like his father Maloji, Shahaji served in the army of Malik Ambar of Ahmadnagar Sultanate.

In 1624 during the Battle of Bhatvadi, Shahaji defeated a combined Mughal-Bijapur force led by the Bijapuri general Mullah Muhammad Lari, by breaching a dam and flooding the Mughal-Bijapur camp. The Marathas portray the battle of Bhatvadi as the beginning of the rise of the Maratha power.

In early 1628, Shahaji returned to Ahmadnagar under the patronage of Malik Ambar's son Fatah Khan.

In 1629, Shahaji led a 6,000-strong cavalry against the Mughals in the Khandesh region, but was defeated.

In 1630, Shahaji's father in-law Lakhuji Jadhavrao, his sons Achloji and Raghoji along with his grandson Yeshwantrao were disarmed and then murdered in the Ahmadnagar court. Therefore, Shahaji defected to the Mughals, along with a 2,000-strong cavalry. The Mughals sent him to occupy Junnar and Sangamner, and gave these districts to him as jagir.

In 1632, Malik Ambar's son Fatah Khan allied with the Mughals. Shahji then left the Mughal service, and returned to Bijapur service.

By 1634, Shahaji had started raiding the area near the Mughal-controlled Daultabad, In the battle of Parenda (1634), the Mughals defeated the Bijapur army led by Shahaji.

Shahaji's jagir in Pune.

As seen in map 1/4 Shahaji's Jagir was the territory between Bhima and Neera, from their source to the confluence. It consisted of twelve Mavals and Pune, Chakan, Sandas, Supe, Shirval, Sasvad, Baramati and Indapur Parganas. Originally these twelve Mavals were the jagir of Randulla khan and the rest was the Jagir of Shahaji.

FIVE PARGANAS AND TWELVE MAVALS

MAP (1/4)

In 1636, Shahaji had surrendered and handed over the Nizam Shah to Randulla Khan, a Bijapuri Sardar. Randulla Khan, on obtaining permission of Adilshah, handed over the Nizam to the Mughals. At the time of treaty, it was decided that Shahaji would hold territories worth twenty-one lakh hon. The area was: Junnar three lakh, Shahgad one lakh, Chakan one lakh, Nashik one lakh, Chambhargonde three to four lakh, Konkan eleven lakh and other small territories three lakh. Besides this, Shahaji was to hold his jagir in Pune. Bara Maval was held perhaps as jagir or otherwise assigned to Randulla Khan by Adilshah. However, within a year, only the jagir of five lakh Hon consisting of Pune, Indapur, Chakan was retained. Junnar, Nashik and all the territories to the North of

Bhima River were taken over by the Mughals and the North Konkan by Adilshah. Shahaji was given an equal jagir in Karnatak.

Map 1/5 shows that at that time, Fateh Khan Siddi of Janjira, an old sardar of Nizamshah was holding the North Konkan secretly on behalf of the heir of Nizamshah and Habashkhan, another Siddi was the protector of this Nizamshahi heir. He was at Mahad. Siddis of Janjira finally got Janjira and Habsan as jagir.

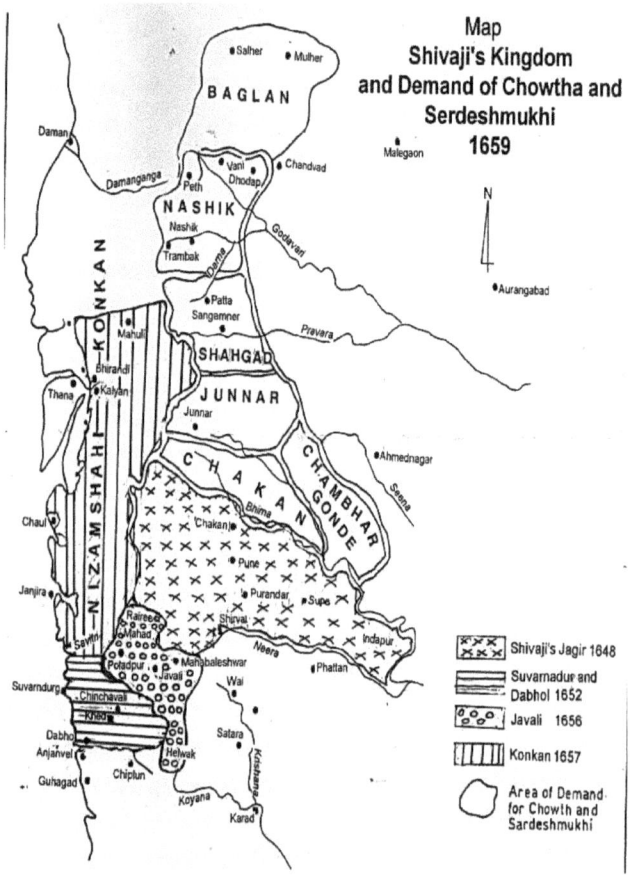

MAP 1/5 Mughalshahi Konkan

Shahaji was allowed to retain his jagir in the Pune region, but was barred from living in that area as part of the Mughal-Bijapur treaty. Therefore, the jagir was placed under the nominal administration of his minor son Shivaji Raje, with his subordinate Dadoji Kondev as its manager. Shahaji himself was transferred to southern part of the Bijapur Sultanate.

The Shivbharat Ch 9/37-44 states that, Shahaji subjugated Veerbhadra king of Bidnur, Keng Naik the rajah of Vrushampattan, Mahabahu Jagdev the rajah of Kaveripattan, Kantirao the rajah of Srirangapattan, Vijayraghav rajah of Tanjavur, Venkatnaik the rajah of Chanji, Trimalnaik the rajah of Madure, Venkatappa the rajah of Pilungad, Srirangraja of Vijayanagar and Tamgauda the rajah of Hansakuta. This made Randulla Khan his general very happy.

In December 1638, Shahaji was also given the charge of Kolar, Hoskote, Doddaballapura, and Sira areas by Ranadulla Khan, in consultation with the Bijapur ruler Muhammad Adil Shah. Shahaji chose Bangalore as his headquarters because of its secure fortress and good climate.

The Bijapur ruler exercised little control over the Bangalore region, and Shahaji ruled the area almost independently. The ruler of Bijapur trusted him, and called him, *the pillar of the state*.

A detailed discussion on Shahaji Raje is beyond the scope of this book. Let us understand that that he realised that he was at best destined to be *Farzand* (son) of the Adishahi while his younger son Shivaji Raje was destined to play major role in Indian if not world History.

So when Adil Shah granted Pune Jagir to Shahaji in 1638, Kanhoji Jedhe and Dadaji Lohkare met Shahaji and they took an oath to establish 'Swarajya'. Their role in the making of Shivaji Raje will be discussed later.

Shivaji Raje 1642-1656.

In 1642 Shahaji Raje sent Jijabai and Shivaji Raje to his jagir at Pune.

Gadhwa Cha Nangar.

(Fig 1 / 6)

On about 1636 on the orders of the Adilshahi, Murarpant burnt the whole Pune area. He also drove an iron rod in the soil and then ploughed the area with an iron plough yoked to a donkey. On that rod he strapped a broken Chappal (footwear)

Legend says that he also planted very destructive babul trees.

Babul (Acacia nilotica (L.) Willd. ex Delile) is a medium sized, thorny, nearly evergreen tree that can reach a height of 20-25 m but may remain a shrub in poor growing conditions. The trunk is short, thick (1 m in diameter) and cylindrical, covered with grey bark. The crown may be flattened or rounded. The leaves are 5-15 cm long, alternate and compound with 7 to 36 pairs of elliptical, 1.5-7 mm long x 0.5-2 mm broad, grey-green, hairy leaflets. Flowers are sweetly scented and bright to golden yellow in colour.

The fruits are linear, flattened, narrow indehiscent pods, 4-22 cm long and 1-2 cm broad, dark-brown to grey in colour and glabrous or velvety. The pods contain 8 to 15 elliptical, flattened bean-shaped dark seeds. Their pods have a characteristic "necklace" shape with constrictions between the seeds.

Fig 1/ 7

Like all other weeds, not only does the Babul tree muscle out all other native species, but also an entire ecosystem of insects, birds and animals which dependent on those trees. Its deep roots, according to some, absorb litres of water, depleting groundwater levels and drying out water bodies.

This was a warning to all concerned that this area is a no-go area. It was a threat that no one should stay and cultivate this land.

Jijamata's Sonyacha Nangar. (Golden Plow)

Jijamata decided to prove that this superstition to be a hoax. As an antidote and to pacify the ryots she had the land ploughed by a *"golden plough"*. It could not be a solid gold plough. Either it must have been gold plated or a piece of gold must have been welded to the plough.

What is more important is that Jijamata announced that those who wished to till the land would be given soft loans to buy seeds and a pair of bullocks. This loan could be repaid over a reasonable period of time. The rate of taxation must be either reduced or even totally abolished. Wolves, wild boar and jackals were a menace. She also announced a cash award for every wolf or jackal that was killed. The ryots were required to submit the tail of the animal to prove he had killed it.

The Kasba Ganpati is the presiding deity of Pune and its history dates back to 400 years. The temple was commissioned by Jijabai, after it was reported to her that an idol of Ganpati had been found in Pune. Although, some claim that the idol was worshipped even before that. The idol was brought by the Thakkar family from Bijapur. Lokmanya Tilak later declared the Kasba Ganpati as the local diety of Pune.

The Kasba Peth (bazaar) was also established by Jijamata.

Social Engineering by Shivaji Raje.

The social background on which Shivaji Raje first worked, and which made his rise to kingship possible and easy, can be clearly pictured form the thousands of family papers of the village headmen of Maharashtra which have been now printed. The Puna district was covered with hundreds of petty masters, each holding a certain village by right or usurpation, and then fighting his neighbouring chieftains or robbing the peasantry around. In that dissolution of civil administration and social order which marked the twilight before the emergence of Shivaji Raje as an independent king, no justice could be had, and no legal right enforced by normal peaceful agency, because such agencies had perished. The strong alone could hold their own, but they did not stop with self-defence and usually turned into usurpers of other people's rights.
On this scene, first Dadaji on a limited scale and then Shivaji Raje in a steadily expanding degree, appeared as the honest judge and strong magistrate. These two alone could be counted upon to give

impartial legal decisions, after following the immemorial custom of consulting a fact - finding jury (mahazar) of local villagers , when disputes about the partition (batni) of ancestral landed property or right to official fees as hereditary revenue-collecting agents or servants of the village community, arose between one family and another, or between brothers and cousins in the same family. Thus Shivaji Raje came to supply a country-wide social need, and his successful rise was due to the moral support which he gained from the public around him . As the fame of his justice, firmness, and stand for the weak was noticed abroad from village to village in Maharashtra, more and more people looked up to him as their protector and longed to come under his rule. His dominion spread first of all through the conquest of hearts which the honest and strong administration alone can achieve among a simple rustic population. And then came his appeal to their individual ambition by providing them with undreamt of opportunities of advancement from the status of common soldiers to that of barons, under his banners. In the end, corporate spirit of the Marathas was kindled and sublimated; they gloried in the evident fact that they were a nation at last rousing itself like a strong man after a long and painful sleep under Muslim tyranny, or like " an eagle mewing its mighty youth". Shivaji Raje succeeded because he was his people' s hero as king.

It was only a " great king " with a compact far-stretching dominion, a body of organised and able civil administrators under his watchful control, and an army strong enough to crush opposition, who could give that security to property and peace in rural society for which every man in Maharashtra was sighing in vain during the agony of the expansion of the rival Muhammadan sultanates of the Deccan or the still greater agony of the dissolution of government during their dying years. That king was Shivaji Raje.

Watandars and Jahgirdars.

The Puna district had many *watandars*, each holding a *watan* (fiefdom) consisting of a few villages. Each watandar sought to increase his watan by fighting his neighbouring watandar and increasing his watan. An increased watan meant more peasants to squeeze from . In this social order might was right. Justice or legal rights did not exist. Shivaji Raje changed all that. Right from Mahabharat disputes about the partition (bantni) of ancestral landed property arose between one families or between brothers was common. Shivaji Raje gave impartial legal decisions, after consulting a fact - finding jury (mahazar) of local villagers.

He had an uncanny knack of seeing the spark in a common foot soldier called *mawala* and upgrading him into a hardened fighter.

The *mawalas* of Mawal displayed courage, perseverance, a stern simplicity, a rough straight forwardness, a sense of social equality and consequently pride in the dignity of man as man. In the seventh century, a learned Chinese traveller thus noted the character of the Maratha people *"The inhabitants are proud-spirited and warlike, grateful for favours and revengeful for wrongs, self-sacrificing towards suppliants in distress and sanguinary to death with any who treated them insultingly."*

Along with courage and endurance, they had the ability to plan and execute surprises and night-attacks, the skill to extricate themselves from a tight corner or vary their tactics according to the changing phases of a battle.

He asked each family to provide him with one son for the cause of Swarajya. *"His readiness to recognize merit, no matter in whom it existed, and to reward it generously drew towards him a large band of brave, intelligent, resourceful men who stood steady fast by his state long after his death."*

The Oath at Rohireshwar 1642-1645.

Young Shivaji Maharaj at a very early age, started gathering influencial Deshmukhs around him like, Baji Pasalkar, Zunzarrao Maral and Haibatrao Shilimkar.

He also formed a firm circle of friends like Chimnaji and Balaji Deshpande (of Shaista strike fame), Yesaji Kank (Elephant Fame) and Kondaji Kank, Suryaji Kakde (of Kanhergad fame) and Trimbak Sondev who were impressed with his frugal living and high thinking.

Fig 1/8

All the above came together on one auspicious day at the sacred Raireshwar Mandir which was situated in the Bhor Taluka. They took an oath to establish Swarajya or self rule.

In 1646 Shivaji Raje took his first step in the establishment of Swarajya by taking Fort Torna. He followed it up by taking Fort Rajgad, Fort Purandar and Fort Kondana (also called Sinhgad).

Along with sagacity, courage and agility the ryots saw a sense of justice and morality in the young Shivaji Maharaj. This was exemplified by punishment given to the Patil of Ranza for molesting a Kunbi (farmhand) girl and the respect shown to the daughter in law of Mulla Ahmed Nawayat of Kalian.

The seal of Shivaji Maharaj.

Two types of official seals were used in Marathi correspondence.

The principal seal, included the name of the person and was at the top of the letter. The closing seal was used to denote closure of the letter and did not include the name of the person. There is a significant factor of Shivaji Raje's seal. Shivaji Raje's Seal is the first seal in Sanskrit, his father Raje's and mother Jijabai's seals are in Pharsi. The earliest available letter by Shivaji Raje is dated 28th January 1646.The seal is at the head of the letter. Shivaji Raje's Seal with its Sanskrit inscription, says. "*This seal of Shahaj's son Shivaji Raje waxing like the crescent of the new moon and revered by the world, shines forth for the welfare of his people*" At the bottom of the letter is the phrase, "maryadeyam virajate" which means 'the letter ends' There are certain significant factors of Shivaji Raje's Seal, Shivaji Raje's Seal is the first seal in Sanskrit, his father Shahaji's and mother Jijabai's seals are in Pharsi.

शिवछत्रपतींची मुद्रा

प्रतिपच्चंद्रलेखेव वर्धिष्णुर्विश्ववंदिता ।
शाहसुनो: शिवस्यैषा मुद्रा भद्राय राजते ॥

Fig 1/ 9

Shivaji Raje's father Shahaji was an important mansabdar of the Adilshahi. In a farman dated 28th March 1644 Shahaji was called *Farzand* ie. son and Maharaj. No other Hindu sardar is known to have been given the title of Maharaja. It is surprising that the son of such a loyal official should have his seal in Sanskrit.

Shivaji Raje's Seal was in use in 1646 i.e., when Shivaji Raje was seventeen years old. It means that by then Shivaji Raje (or his parents and teachers) had decided on the course of his life before that.

All the seals of the astapradhans sardars and officials of Shivaji Raje are in Sanskrit proving that it was not a whim or fancy but conceived with purpose and intent.

The Early Days.

W C Bendre writes *"Sevagy had not completed twelve when his father gave him the command of 300 sawars. As Sevagy was so young, he gave him as his tutor an old soldier and near relative called Neotogey .... who knew that Sevagy was not only quick in action but lively in carriage also, for with a clear and fair face, nature had given him the greatest perfections, specially the dark big eyes were so lively that they seemed to dart rays of fire. To these was added a quick, clear and acute intelligence.*

At this time two parganas, named Puna and Supa became the jagir of Shahji Bhosla, Sevagy became the Manager of these two parganas on the part of his father, and looked carefully after them. He was distinguished in his tribe for his courage and intelligence; and for craft and trickery he was reckoned a sharp son of the devil the father of fraud. In that country where all the hills rise to the sky, and the jungles are full of trees and bushes, he had an inaccessible abode. Like the zamindars of the country, he set about erecting forts on hills, and mud forts, which in the Hindavi dialect of the Dakhin are called Garhi. "

Whenever he heard of a prosperous town, or of a district inhabited by thriving cultivators, he plundered it and took possession of it. Before the Jagirdars in those troublous times could tell to Bijapur, he had sent in his own account of the matter, with present and offerings, charging the Jagirdars or proprietors with some offence which he had felt called upon to punish, and offerings to pay some advanced amount for the lands on their being attached to his own Jagir, and to pay their revenues direct to the government. He communicated these matters to the officials at Bijapur, who in those disturbed times took little heed of what any one did. So when the Jagirdar's complaints arrived, he obtained no redress, because no one could take any notice of it."

"From here Sevagy passed to Bhiundim (Bhiwandi) and Galiana (Kalyan), 14 leagues to the north, all the way through the territories of the Great Mogol, destroying till he reached the above mentioned cities. He suddenly appeared in Galiana and robbed immense amount of wealth, for it was the home of great

merchants. At the same time when Galiana was sacked, he ordered an attack on Bhiundim, three leagues from the other city, where he repaired in person when there was nothing more to be got at Galiana, He remained longer in Bhiundim to work some wonders. He not only robbed what the inhabitants possessed but also great treasures of which they were ignorant. They were reasonable surprised that a stranger should dig from earth (things) of which the oldest of them knew nothing even by tradition......In this manner great treasures that were hidden and totally unknown were openly removed."

Aurangzeb's Second Viceroyality 1652-1658.

In 1652 the Mughal prince Aurangzeb became viceroy of the Deccan and Dara Shukoh his elder brother was sent to recapture Kandahar. Murad was in Gujrat and Shuja was in Bengal.

Fig1/ 10 Aurangzeb

As we saw, the Deccan was a poor province, with erratic rains, sterile soil and uninterested cultivators. It had the Nizamshahi and Beradshahi on the southern borders and that required a standing army .Since the revenue fell short of expenses, the annual deficit being Rs 20,36,000, grants were required from Malwa and Gujarat in order to maintain the administration. This situation was a result of ten years of an incompetent jagirdars, depopulation, famine and war. To make matters worse, Shah Jahan goaded Aurangzeb that things could be improved, if efforts were made to develop agriculture. It must be remembered that by now Shah Jahan had already anointed Dara Shikoh as the heir apparent. Shah Jahan was only trying to demoralize and put down Aurangzeb.

Accordingly, Aurangzeb appointed Murshid Quli Khan to introduce the zabt revenue system of northern India based on the system of Raja Todarmal. To increase revenue, Murshid Quli Khan granted loans for seed, livestock, and irrigation infrastructure.

Aurangzeb tightened the administration, started weeding out corrupt officials, visited each fort, inspected grain and ammunition, dismissed or retired incompetent clerks and soldiers.

The Deccan slowly and steadily returned to prosperity.

Aurangzeb's Invasion Of Bijapur

On 04 Nov 1656, Mohamed Adilshah died without a heir. His queen Badi Begam Sahiba Tajul Mukhdirat placed a boy from his harem, Ali Adilshah on the throne.

In order to resolve the financial situation Aurangzeb advanced against the Sultan of Bijapur.

On 26 Nov1656, Aurangzeb asked permission from Shah Jahan to invade Bijapur. It was granted.

On 28 Feb 1657, Shah Jahan sent an army of 20 thousand under Mir Jumla

On 2 March 1657, Mir Jumla lays seige to Bidar Fort.

On 29 March1657, Mughals commenced an artillary attack. The Killedar (commander) of the fortified city, Sidi Marjan, was mortally wounded when a gunpowder magazine exploded.

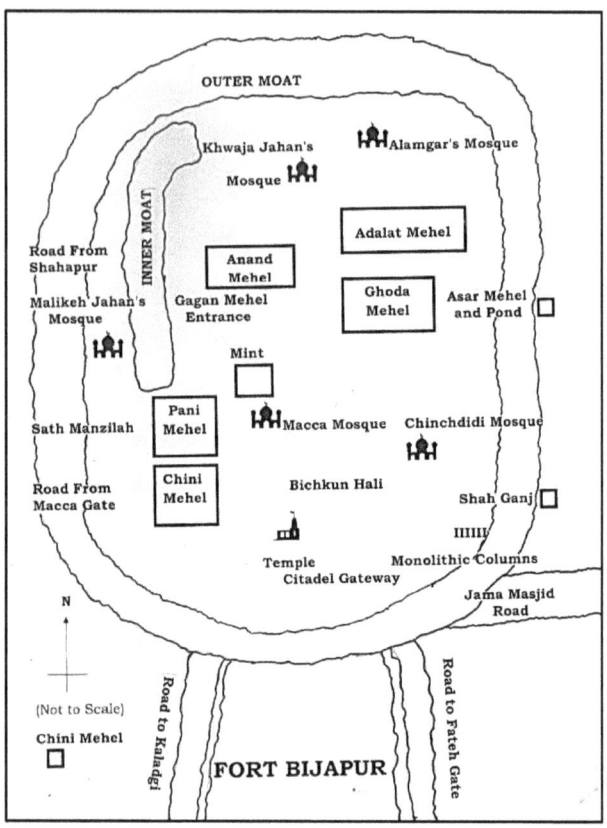

Fig 1/ 11

After twenty-seven days of hard fighting, Bidar was captured by the Mughals and Aurangzeb continued his advance.

Mughals gained a large booty of 12 lakhs in cash, Rs eight lakhs worth gun powder and 250 cannon balls.

Battle Of Kalyani-Bidar.

The battle of Kalyani-Bidar took place on 1657 between 15,000 Mughals led by Aurangzeb and 20,000 Adilshahi led by Siddi Marjan. Kaliany fell on 29 July 1657. But Bijapur started negotiations with Emperor through Dara Shukoh.

The terms of Treaty between Shah Jahan and Adilshah -

1-Adilshahi ceded forts of Parinda, Bidar and Kalyani with their dependent territories.

2-War indemnity of one crore rupees.

3- Aurangzeb was ordered to make peace and return to Bidar.

Aurangzeb was frustrated that Shah Jahan chose to settle for negotiations with the opposing forces, rather than pushing for complete victory.

Again, he was sure that Dara had exerted influence on his father. In this way Dara got the credit for being a diplomate of peace while Aurangzeb was labelled a war monger.

On 6 sept 1657, Shah Jahan fell ill.

On 4 oct 1657, Aurangzeb began his retreat from Kalyani and proceeds North to take part in the War of Succession.

Mughal war of Succession.

A discussion on the Mughal war of succession is beyond the scope of this book.

We shall describe in brief how Aurangzeb came to power.

1. Battle of Bahadurpur (16/02/1658) Suleman Shikoh (son of Dara) defeated Shuja
2. Battle of Dharmat (15/04/1658) Aurangzeb and Murad defeated the Mughal Imperial army led by Jaswant Singh.
3. Battle of Samuhgad (29/05/1658) Aurangzeb and Murad defeated Dara Shikoh.
4. Battle of Khajwa (05/01/1659) Aurangzeb defeated Shuja.
5. Battle of Deorai (13 /03/1659) Aurangzeb defeated Dara.

On 21 July 58, the first coronation of Aurangzeb took place.

Shahaji disowns Shivaji Raje.

Sabhasad says seeing that Shivaji Raje was defiant in taking on the Adilshahi and the speed at which he was capturing fort after fort, it was imperative for Shahaji to distance himself from Shivaji Raje's actions. Shahaji had informed the Adilshah that he had disowned his wife and son, that they did not obey him and that the Adilshah was free to deal with them as he deemed fit.

At first Adilshah had accepted this position and had agreed not to hold Shahaji accountable, as is seen from the following farman.

Ali Adilshah to Shahaji :

"Be it known to Maharaja Farzand Shahji Bhosale:

"Of late, an apprehension has been created in your mind that the blame for the treason and arrogance of Shivaji Bhosale might be laid on your head. However, let it be known to you that we are fully cognizant of his improper expressions and actions. You are therefore wholly unconnected with them. The responsibility of his transgressions and crimes rests upon him alone. So keep your mind completely composed in this regard.

"Our grace rests upon you in greater measure than in the past. As a token thereof, we are bestowing on you your entire previous jagir. There would be no change therein. We also command that the chieftains in the vicinity of the Bangalore Fort should maintain relations with you.

" Any person expressing anything adverse about you will be subject to our wrath."

Several other supporting reference may be cited for the fact that Shahji had disowned all responsibility for Shivaji Raje's actions. The Shivabharat recounts a speech attributed to Ali Adilshah just before Afzal Khan left Bijapur on his campaign against Shivaji in 1659 in which there appears the following remark:
" His father Shahji, too, is incapable of instructing that arrogant person [i.e. Shivaji Raje]". This suggests that Shahji had been exonerated from all responsibility for his son's actions.

However as we shall see later Adilshah changed his mind and imprisoned Shahaji.

The Portuguese governors, Françesco de Melo de Castro and Antonio da Souza Coutinho, in their letter dated 15 May 1658 to their king, state that " *Shivaji... dose not obey his father."*

Niccolao Manucci a Venetian traveler states in the Storia do Mogor:

" Shivaji Raje... lived in the family territory while his father was at the court, and began to realize money without sending any to the father. Next he began to enlist men and attack the lands of Bijapur in all directions, giving no heed to either his father or the king. The latter complained to Shahji of Shivaji Raje's temerity, and Shahji replied that his Majesty might act as he pleased. His son neither obeyed him nor remitted to him revenues of their lands, and had already declared himself a rebel to the crown."

CHAPTER TWO

Jawli 1656.

At the extreme north-western corner of the Satara lies Jawli, which consisted of eighteen valleys (*khores*) ie Jambhul, Jor, Shivthar, Kandat, Tam, Bamnoli, Atgaon, Chatwarbet, Solas. The subdivision of Jawli is "*throughout hilly and thickly wooded with evergreen trees..... The narrow rugged and steep crest of the Sahyadris rising 4,000 feet or more above sea-level forms its western wall; and in the valleys the tree growth is luxuriant forming high forests* " Within a length of 100 km as many as eight passes cross the range and transported a large trade from the Deccan plateau to Mahad in Kolaba and Chiplun in Ratnagiri.

The Mores

Legend says that the jungle in Jawli was so dense that *'one could find a lice in the fur of a bear, but you cannot find an elephant in Jawli'*

Since eight generations a Maratha family named the More had received a grant of the state of Jawli from the sultan of Bijapur. The head of the family bore the hereditary title of Chandra Rao and had a standing army of 12,000.

As seen above, the region was inaccessible, therefore the Adishahi government did not interfere with the day to day working of Jawli. The Mores were free to govern at will as long as they paid tribute to Adilshahi. As with all fiefdoms, Chandrarao was the head of the family and all the other members of the family ruled various parts of the fief in a subordinate capacity.

In about 1648, Daulatrao Chandrarao More had died without leaving behind him a heir.

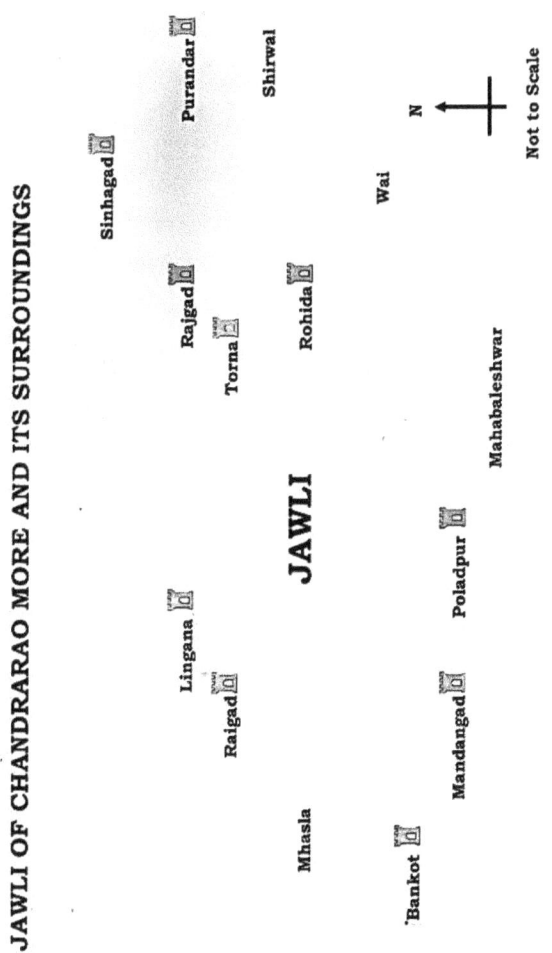

Fig 2 / 1

As is usual in such a case, each male from the family laid claim to the title of Chandrarao. The widow of Daulatrao had adopted a boy from the family of the Mores of Shivthar and had pleaded with Shivaji Raje to assist her to secure his accession to the estate. Shivaji Raje saw to it that her protégé was made the chief of the estate, however the disputes in the family continued to simmer.

The campaign against the Mores

In 1649 Afzal Khan was appointed as the Governor of the Wai province by the Bijapur Government. He came to know of disputes in the More family. By then Afzal Khan was at loggerheads with the Bhosle family. A protégé of Shivaji Raje sitting on the throne of Jawli was unacceptable to him. Afzal khan decided to intervene in the Jawli affairs. However Afzal Khan was posted in the Karnatak campaigns and there was a status co.

As we saw earlier from 1646 Shivaji Raje took his first step in the establishment of Swarajya by taking Fort Torna. He followed it up by taking Fort Rajgad, Fort Purandar and Fort Kondana (also called Sinhgad). With the Mughals involved in the war of succession and Adilshahi involved with the Karnataka campaign, Shivaji Raje was keen to expand his kingdom.

Map 1/5 shows that

1.To the west of his Pune Jahgir was the Nizamshahi area taken over by the Mughals.

2-To the North East was the Adil Shahi area taken over by the Mughals.

Since Shivaji Raje did not wish to take on the mighty Mughals immediately, the area to the South West of his kingdom ie Jawli beckoned him as we saw Chandrarao owed his position to Shivaji Maharaj, but instead of being grateful to him he became jealous and hostile. He treated Shivaji Raje as an upstart and scornfully turned down his demand that he should be subordinate to him. Infact instead of joining Shivaji Raje in his clarion call for Swarajya, Chandra Rao tried to form an anti-Shivaji alliance with the help of the Adil Shahi governor, because Shivaji Raje became a direct threat to More's eight generation unrestricted power and independence.

More Objects To Shivaji Raje.

Shivaji Raje could no longer tolerate the arrogant and defiant attitude of the Mores. Unlike the other Maval Deshmukhs, the Mores like many other Maratha Sardars were satisfied being the vassals of the Adilshahi.

To them *Swarajya was a vague,* strange and impossible idea.

In about end of 1655, Shivaji Raje sent a message, to Chandrarao More:

"You call yourself a king (Raja). I am a king. Shri Shambhu Mahadeva has given me sovereignty. You should not in future entitle yourself a Raja. Come and be my vassal. If not I will attack Jawli and arrest you."

Chandrarao replied, *"You have become a king only yesterday. Who has bestowed upon you this sovereignty ? If you have any courage in you, you should meet us today and not postpone the visit till tommorrow. I have been appointed king by the Badshah (Adilshah). We have been kings of Jawli for (eight) generations. If you wish to confront us, think (before). Instead of success you will find only failure."*

An enraged Shivaji Raje then sent one more letter,

"Give up Jawli, stop calling yourself king, tie your hands in a handkerchief and serve huzur (throne). If you resist you shall be killed ."

Needless to say Chandrarao remained obstinate. He wrote,

"My gunpowder is ready. You have sent some irresponsible letters. How did you have the temerity to write such letters ?"

Sabhasad says, Shivaji Raje deputed Raghunath Ballal Korde to attack and eliminate Chandrarao More. He said,*"Unless Chandra Rao More is killed, the kingdom cannot be gained. None but you can do this deed. I will send you to him as my envoy."*

Raghunath Ballal Korde went to Jawli as an envoy and started peace negotiation with Chandra Rao. Raghunath Ballal Korde was not a Maratha and therefore not one of the known aggressive sardars of Shivaji Raje. He was accompanied by a small band of people who looked like clerks rather than swordsmen.

On 14 January 1656, the first day the usual formal diplomatic talks took place and gifts were exchanged. Raghunath Ballal Korde confirmed what Shivaji Raje's spies had informed him, that Chandra Rao lived a grandiose and luxurious life. Since no one had attacked a Chandrarao for eight generations he led a carefree and lax life. Raghunath knew Chandrarao was a sitting duck.

On 15 January 1656, on the second day Raghunath seemed to agree with all that Chandra Rao demanded, when he suddenly drew his dagger and stabbed Chandra Rao to death. At the same time the envoys accompanying him killed his brother Surya Rao. After the elimination of Chandrarao, the diplomatic envoys became menacing swordsmen who made short work of the stunned and careless guards.

Quickly they went to the rendezvous where Shivaji Raje was waiting stealthily in the dense forest of Jawli.

The surprised guards made a hue and cry and that was the signal for Shivaji Raje to assault Jawli in full strength. The More family made a vain attempt to defend themselves but soon Chandra Rao's two sons and the entire family fled to a tall mountain named Rairi. (this same Rairi later became the invincible Raigad Fort)

Only Hanumant Rao of the More family put up a spirited fight. Shivaji Raje realised that "unless he eliminated Hanumant, the thorn would not be removed from Jawli."

So, he sent Shambhuji Kavji with a pretended proposal for the hand of Hanumant Rao's daughter. Hanumant was dumbfounded at the proposal and before he could react he was stabbed to death.

Under the rule of the More's, the administration of Jawli had deteriorated. Shivaji Raje took about six weeks, to settle the affairs of Jawli and appointed competent officers to ensure the safety of his newly capture province.

On about 30 March 1656, after ensuring that there was no chance of a surprise attack on Jawli, Shivaji Raje turned his attention to Rairi where the late Chandra Rao More's sons Krishnaji and Baji had taken refuge.

Rairi was a very lofty and inaccessible plateau, of which Henry Oxiden later wrote *'we arrived at the top of that strong mountain which is more fortified by nature than art, being of very difficult access but only one avenue to it, which is guarded by two narrow gates and fortified by with a strong high wall and bastions thereto, all the other part of the mountaine is a direct precipice so that it is impregnable, except the Treachery of some in it betrays it.'*

Chandra Rao More's sons Krishnaji and Baji were young and inexperienced and they tamely surrendered on April 1656.

So far Shivaji Raje's victories were restricted to a few forts but after the capture of Jawli three developments took place.

1-More's army of 10,000 passed into Shivaji Raje's hands doubling its strength. Many of Chandra Rao More's brave officers like Murar Baji and his brothers Trimbakji, Shankarji, Sambhaji and Mahadji along with Tanaji Malusare joined Shivaji Raje. As we shall see later Murar Baji excelled himself at the Battle of Chakan and Tanaji Malusare at the Battle of Sinhgad/Kondana.

2- Shivaji Raje was free to invade South Konkan with ease or extend his dominion southwards into the Kolhapur district westwards.

Therefore Shivaji Raje struck. It was a bitter but straight fight and the aim of Shivaji Raje was the annexation of the region.

The exact words of the Jedhe Karina are *"The lord (Shivaji Raje) sent Raghunath Ballal Sabnis from Poona with a force of Cavalry. He killed Hanumatrao and captured Zor."*

The Sanskrit poem Suryavansham says '*Shivaji Raje gained Jawli after slaying in battle Baji Raj and Krishna Raj and their father Chandra Raj that he also slew Chandra Raj's helpers and relatives ie Hanumant Rao More and that Pratap Varma the bandhav brother of Chandra Rao fled and later joined Afzal Khan'.*

After the annexation of Jawli, Shivaji Maharaj ordered Moropant Pingle to build a new fort on the hill named Bhorpya and named it Pratapgarh, the actual work was done by Arjoji Yadav an architect. Here he set up an image of his patron goddess Bhavani, as the more ancient Bhavani of Tuljapur was too far away. Pratapgad is at a height of 3000 M, its area is 300X400 M and it looks like -a butterfly

Tulja Bhawani

GODDESS BHAVANI OF PRATAPGAD

Fig 2/ 2

Tulja Bhavani is a form of goddess Parvati, who is worshiped in Maharashtra, and also by people of Telangana, Northern Karnataka, and Nepal. "Bhavani" translates to "giver of life", meaning the power of nature or the source of creative energy. She is considered to be a mother who provides to her devotees and also plays the role of dispensing justice by killing Asuras.

The history of the temple dates back to the days of ' Skanda Purana ' as it finds a mention in that holy script. According to the epic story, there was a sage "Kardam" and his consort "Anubhuthi' with an infant, in this area. After his death his wife "Anubhuthi" performed a penance for goddess in the name of Bhavani on the banks of river "Mandakini" to look after her child. There was a demon (Rakshasa) by name "Kukur" who tortured her. Then Goddess Bhavani rescued Anubhuthi and killed the demon. The goddess on the prayer of her pet devotee settled on the hill of "Bala ghat". Since then the Mother Goddess came to be called as Bhavani of Tuljapur or Tulja Bhavani.

It is second among of the 51 Shakti Peetas attributed to Goddess Parvati.

Tuljapur is at 45 km from Solapur. The Goddess is said to be swayambhu (self-emanated). It is true that God or Goddess is always referred as 'swayambhu' in Vedas, Puranas and many legends. But it does not refer to the stone idol installed in a temple. What is attributed is to the invisible Supreme power.

It is the family deity of the Bhosale Royal family, the Yadavs and of countless numbers of families belonging to different castes.

Shivaji Raje's status after Jawli

On 24 September 1656, Shivaji Raje paid a friendly visit to Supa, and surprised its captain Shambhuji Mohite during a festival celebration.

As seen in the Maps 1 /4 and 2/ 1 the possession of Supa, Baramati and Indapur rounded off the south-eastern corner of the Puna district, while the acquisition of Purandar, Raigarh, Kondana, Rohida and Torna secured Shivaji Raje's territory by a strong chain of hill-forts on the south. North -west of Puna he acquired the forts of Tikona, Lohgarh, and Rajmachi, the last of which stood on the Sahyadri crest (10 km north of the Bhor pass) and overlooked the Konkan plain on the west.

Passes of Jawli

One of the sources of income of the More's had been the toll from passes on the goods that came from the sea ports and went to Pune, Ahmednagar, Satara, Kolhapur, Bijapur and Golkonda. These passes were Kevnale, Kinsar, Shetrapal, Kumte, Dhavle, Kadnali, Sapalkhind, Karje, Hatlot, Parghat. It must be understood that loosing Jawli was death blow to the Mores but loosing the control over the passes struck a body blow to the Adilshahi treasury.

It must be remembered that, during period of January 1656 while Shivaji Raje was involved with the Jawli affair, Afzal Khan was involved with the siege of Parenda.

Shivaji's officers

A Mahzar, (document) embodying proceedings and conclusion in a dispute about the Deshmukhi watan of Poona dated March 21,1657, record the names of Shivaji Raje's officers who were present at the meeting. Shivaji Raje himself was present during the proceedings. The officers of Shivaji Raje are as follows. Shamraj Nilkanth -the Peshwa, Wasudeva Balkrishna, the Muzumdar, Sonaji Vishwanath -the Dabir, Mahadaji Shamraj -the Surnis, Mankoji Dahatonde -the Sarnobat, Raghunath Ballal - the Sabnis, Noorbeg - the Sarnobut of the Infantry and Shamraj Padmanabhi - the Sabnis of the Infantry. Netoji Palkar was an early adherent of Shivaji Raje. In addition to the above, new names began to appear among the followers of Shivaji Raje. (1) Anaji Rangnath Molkare was appointed Sabnis for the fort of Purandar, sometime in 1654.

(2) Moropant Pingle had early joined Shivaji Raje and was busy constructing the Pratapgad fort.

(3) Abaji Mahadev had joined Shivaji Raje soon after 1649. He worked as Shivaji Raje's envoy (*hejib*) and was soon to be appointed as (1657) Governor of Kalyan.

(4) The brothers Abaji Sondev and Nilo Sondev were also early adherents of Shivaji Raje.

(5) Krishnaji Bhaskar was Shivaji Raje's officers in charge of the Mawals. He is to be distinguished from the Krishnaji Bhaskar who was from wai and was a messanger from Afzalkhan.

(6) Gomaji Naik Pansambal had attached himself to the Bhosles at the time of Jijabai's marriage to Shahaji . He was one of the trusted adherents of Shivaji Raje. (7) Pantaji Gopinath Bokil was Kulkarni of the village of Hivre and seems to have been in the service of Shivaji Raje since at least 1630.

(8) Phirangoji Narsala, the custodian of the fort of Chakan was formerly an officer under Shahaji and continued under Shivaji Raje.

(9) Baji Gholap was appointed custodian of the fort of Purandar after its capture by Shivaji Raje in 1654.

(10) Sambhaji Kavji Kondhalkar, took part in Shivaji Raje's campaign against the Mores.

(11) Tanaji Malusare was from Umrat and must have entered Shivaji Raje's service after the latter's campaign against the Mores.

Aurangzeb warns about Shivaji Raje

In 1658 before going to the North, Aurangzeb, had instructed his officers in the following manner. *"Village Headsman and people of our territory, who had secretly helped Shivaji Raje should be killed without mercy....." "Villages in Shivaji Raje's territory should be ruined without any mercy and people should be killed and looted fully." "Shivaji Raje's Pune and Chakan should be burnt down. Kill all the inhabitants and make them slaves, people should be made to desert all the villages, they should be thoroughly looted and killed.*" In any case Shivaji Raje continued his activities unabated. When Adilshah later enquired with Shahaji Raje, he had replied *"...My son does not listen to me. Adilshah can deal with him any way he desires."*

Adilshah is also credited to have said "......*Father cannot be held responsible for son...*"

Aurangzeb's Letter To Shivaji Raje

In February 1658, when Aurangzeb had left the Deccan to fight for the throne, Shivaji Raje had sent him a letter, expressing his repentance over the 'crimes' he had committed. In reply Aurangzeb addresses Shivaji Raje by the epithet *'Multi-ul Islam'*, which means *"one who is obedient to Islam"*,

The letter reads:

"Your petition sent with your envoy, Raghunath Pandit, was placed before us along with the letter addressed to Krishna Pandit Bhaskar."

"Your offences are too numerous to merit our forgiveness, but you have expressed a desire for rendering loyal service to us and are repenting over your misdeeds. Because our court is not oblivious to such sincerity, your crimes have been forgiven on the condition of your commitment to adhere to the means of attaining fortune. Strive hard to manifest it."

"You have requested that if you are granted all the territories of your watan, along with the territories and forts in the Konkan, after the old Nizamshahi territory which now belongs to Adil Khan comes into possession of the imperial officials, you would send Sona Pandit to our court, and, once you receive our letter granting your request, you would assign an officer with a contingent of not less than 500 troopers to our services, besides co-operating with Imperial officials for protection of our borders, and would not allow the dust of rebellion to rise in the land in any way."

Therefore, the order is:

"You will conduct yourself in strict accordance with your assurance. Immediately upon receipt of this letter, send us a written request with Sonaji stating your demands and requests, so that they may be granted. Consider this as a strict warning to you not to stray from the royal road of loyalty."

"Be it known that our grace rests upon you."

Written on 24th February 1658.

"[Post Script] Jaswant Singh and Qasim Khan were at Ujjain with a force of 25,000 troopers and a large part of artillery. When they learned of our advance to 6 kos from Ujjain, they insolently came forward to give us battle, but they were soundly beaten, lost five or six thousand troopers, and fled away. Their camp with its entire treasury, artillery, elephants and other valuables was plundered. Thus, thanks to God, a great victory was attained.

"By the grace of God, we shall soon achieve new victories, so that the wishes of all loyalists and well-wishers would be fulfilled and the enemies will experience frustration.

"You should experience greater joy and exultation by these happy tidings and adhere to the straight path of loyalty and hope for rewards in proportion to your fidelity."

The above post script refers to the Battle of Dharmat described earlier as a part of the War of succession.

The letter talks about the territory that Shivaji Maharaj had brought under his control in the Konkan which had been in the possession of the Nizamshah and was annexed by the Adilshah in conformity with the terms of the treaty of 1636 between himself and the Mughals. After the new treaty of 1657, this region was actually to be delivered to the Mughals. But it was amply clear by now that the Adilshah was not likely to honour the commitment. In any case, Shivaji Raje had by this time captured most of that territory, in spite of which Shivaji Raje sent a written request to Aurangzeb to let him keep it! (Map 1/5) However Aurangzeb was not naïve. He knew exactly what Shivaji Maharaj was up to.

On 10 May 1657, Aurangzeb wrote to Naziri Khan *'the accursed Shiva(ji) should be punished for his audacity and insolence.*

On 10 Oct 1657, he wrote to Naziri Khan *"that ill-fated one must be completely uprooted. Having rebelled he should be plundered, invaded and his territory despoiled. If he steps forward for a conflict, deflate his ego with your sword and punish him suitably."*

Aurangzeb advices Adilshah on Shiva(ji).

On 5 February 1658, Aurangzeb left the Deccan to contest the throne. Before leaving for Delhi, Aurangzeb gave some advice to Adilshah.

"Be diligent. Protect this country, expel Shiva,

The son of a dog is waiting for an opportunity"

"If you desire to enlist the services of the evil intentioned and accursed Shiva, who has trespassed upon some forts in the Konkan and raised the dust of rebellion, be sure to assign a jagir in Karnataka so that he will be far away from the Imperial territory and will be unable to incite a revolt."

Adilshah now decided to turn his undivided attention to Shivaji Raje. The Tarikh-i-Ali records it as follows.

"He (Shivaji Raje) was extending the hand of repression and injustice like a greedy and hungry dog, that does not feel satisfied with the bone it gets and wants more and was oppressing the faithful (Muslims) who were engrossed in prayer.

Shahaji Bhosle and his eldest son Sambhaji.

It is worth noting that in 1638 the Adilshah sent Afzal Khan and Kenge Hanuappa Nayak.against Bangalore. On the way they decided to attack Sira which was ruled by Kasturi Ranga. When Kasturi Ranga came to know of this attack on his kingdom, he realized that he was no match for the army of Afzal Khan. He asked for a meeting to decide the terms of the treaty. During the interview Afzal Khan killed him alleging that Kasturi Ranga had intended to betray his trust.

Of course, this was a lie and Sir Jadunath Sarkar puts it best.

'A defeated and submissive chieftain, away from his own army and unarmed does not attempt murder in his enemy's den. He humbly seeks peace by every means in his power.'

Shahaji and Jijabai had an eldest son named Sambhaji. He was a full-blown adult warrior in 1654 because he was part of the

Kanakgiri siege and without his father Shahaji. The Chitnis Bakhar states that during the siege of Kanakgiri, Afzal Khan took a bribe from the ruler of Kanakgiri and did not send the promised re-enforcements to Sambhaji. In the ensuing one-sided skirmish thst followed Sambhaji was felled by a cannon shot.

Both Shahaji Raje and Jijabai never forgot nor forgave Afzal Khan for this treachery.

As if this were not enough the following passage will explain why the very mention of Afzal Khan raised the hackles of Shivaji Raje and Jijabai.

In 1648 Mustafa Khan an Adilshahi wazir had laid siege to Jinji in Tamilnadu. Shahaji Raje was one of the mansabdars under his command.

In the middle of the siege Shahaji Raje requested for permission to withdraw with his force to his jagir. Mustafa Khan refused. Adilshah asked Mustafa Khan to arrest Shahaji Raje. But Mustafa Khan had pledged friendship with Shahaji Raje and even sworn by his son's (Atish) head.

The Shivbharat Ch 11/24-28 says :

Mustafa Khan came forward a long distance to receive Shahaji Raje, clasped his hand tightly, showed his happiness, smiled at him, showed his affection, showered gifts on him, praised him, joked and jested with him, spoke about philosophy, his well being day after day and thus gained his confidence and trust. But a servant had to obey his master, and the master (Adilshah) had commanded him to imprison Shahaji Raje.

A night of merriment and revelry followed, the owls, elephants, dogs and horses became alarmed, lightening and whirlwind followed.

Diler Khan, Masud Khan, Yakut Khan, Farad Khan, Kairat Khan, Kut Khan, Azam Khan, Raian Khan, along with Raghav Mambaji, Vedoji Bhaskar, Mambaji Pawar, Baji Ghorpade surrounded the camp of the sleeping Shahaji and arrested him (while his horse was bare of the saddle and the elephant was devoid of the hauda).

Four factors contributed to Shahaji's arrest. His friction with Mustafa Khan, his increasing hold over the mansabdars in Karnataka, his own ambitions and aspirations. However, it would be correct to say that Shivaji Raje capturing Konadana in 1647 was the proverbial last straw.

Arrest of Shahaji

A very reliable Persian history of Bijapur, viz., Basatin-us-salatin, supplies the following information:- *"Shahaji, withdrawing his head from obedience to the Nawab Mustafa Khan, began to oppose him, till at last the Nawab decided to arrest him. One day he sent Bajirao Ghorpade and Jaswant Rao very early in the morning to Shahaji's camp. Shahaji, having passed the preceding night in mirth and reveiry, was still sleeping in bed. As soon as the two arrived and he learnt of their purpose, he in utter bewilderment took horse and galloped away from his house alone. Baji Ghorpade gave chase, caught him, and brought him before the nawab, who threw him into confinement. His contingement of 3,000 cavalry was dispersed, and his camp was thoroughly looted. Adil Shah on hearing of it sent from his court Afzal Khan to bring Shahaji away and an eunuch to attach his property."*

On 25 July 1648, this news of Shahaji Raje's arrest reached his eldest son Sambhaji, and his younger son Shivaji Raje.

Along with Shahaji Raje, Kanhoji Jedhe and Dadaji Lohkare with his son Ratnajipant Lohkare were also arrested at Kanakgiri.

Though captive Shahaji Raje after coming to Adilshahi, was not illtreated but placed under the care, of an eminent umrao named Ahmad Khan with instructions to not harm him in any way.

Battle of Purandar (1648-49)

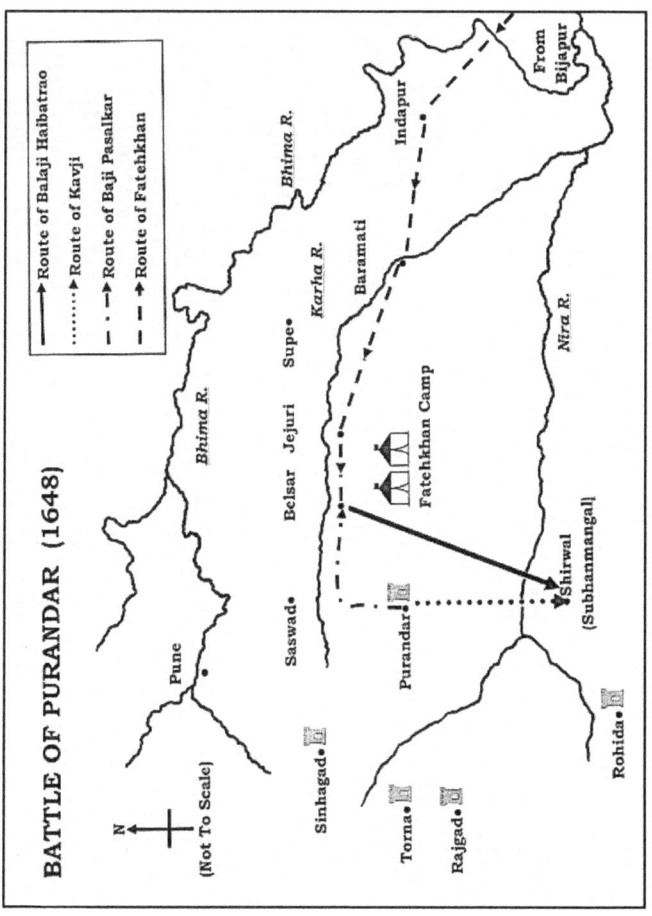

Map 2/ 3

After the arrest of Shahaji, Mustafa Khan sent a force against Shivaji Raje under the command of Fateh Khan. The force was about 4000 to 5000 strong. Shivbharat gives us the names of officers ie Minad Khan, Ratan Shaikh, Ashraf Shah, Musa Khan Fazil shah, Mataji Ghatge, Bajaji Nimbalkar and Balaji Haibatrao.

Fateh Khan pitched his camp at Belsar, 15 km east of Purandar.

The Shivbharat says in Ch 13, that on October 1648 Fateh Khan led the Bijapuri forces against Shivaji Raje, accompanied by Minhaji Shaikh, Ratan Shaikh, Fateh Khan, Sharaf Shah, Ghatge, Baji Naik and Ballal Haibatrao. They attacked and captured Shirwal.

Shivaji Raje decided to recapture Shirwal and he sent his troops under Kalji, Godaji Jagtap, Bhimaji Wagh, Sambhaji Kate, Shiwaji Ingle, Bhikaji Chor and his brother Bhairav. Takaji and Sadoji and rest of Shivaji Maharaj's forces attacked the strongly held fort and after a desperate struggle, captured it. In the battle the Bijapuri commandant, Ballal was killed.

On hearing of the capture of Shirwal by Shivaji Raje, Fateh Khan decided to attack Shivaji Raje near Purandar.

Musa khan was in the vanguard, the Rajah of Phaltan was posted to the left wing, while the right wing was guarded by Ghatge. Fateh khan was in the rear The attack was met with a vigorous resistance. It was a hand to hand fight. After a desperate struggle the Bijapuri forces broke and fled the field, leaving behind them a number of dead and wounded. Fateh Khan's captain, Musa Khan was among the slain.

In this fight Shivaji Raje's men greatly distinguished themselves. Baji, the son of Kanhoji Jedhe who had joined Shivaji Raje, fought desperately and triumphantly brought back the standard which was at one time in danger of being snatched away by the enemy., Shivaji Raje conferred on Baji the title of *Sarjerao* for his gallantry. in this fight Shivaji Raje lost Baji Pasalkar, the Deshmukh of Muse Khore and a valued colleague.

Standard /Flags

Flags are an insignia of leadership, serving for the identification of friend or foe and as rallying points.

They were to be treated with a level of respect similar to that given to the ruler.

They are a symbol of pride and members of the army have laid down their lives to keep the flag flying in its full glory.

If in skirmish, the enemy takes possession of the flag or standard it a sign of insult and loss of honour.

Shivaji Raje corresponds with Shehzada Murad Baksh

Although the Mughals maintained peace with Bijapur for a period of twenty years following the year 1636, they were eager to seduce Bijapuri officials from their allegiance and entertain them in their service.

Shivaji Raje was aware of this. Therefore when in March 1649 Shahaji Raje was arrested and brought in chains from Jinji to Bijapur. Shivaji Raje petitioned the Mughal prince Murad Bakhsh the Viceroy of the Deccan.

On 14 March 1649, Murad Bakhsh replied to Shivaji Raje.

Shivaji Bhonsla, know that the letter professing extreme devotion that you sent me has been placed before me. In the matter of your coming to my presence, you have begged for a letter from me summoning you and giving you assurances of safety. It is the practice of true loyalty that you should first of send to me a high envoy of yours, who may be relied upon so that I may learn of your intentions and demands, and send you (in return) a princely letter of conciliation stamped with the impression of my palm and accompanied by many favours. Keep your mind composed in all respects and send your envoy quickly....."

It is interesting to note that even after the release of Shahaji Raje there was correspondence between Shivaji and Murad Bakhsh, as the following letters show.

On 14 August 1649, Prince Murad Bakhsh wrote to Shivaji Raje, " *Shivaji Bhonsla....Be glorified with our boundless princely favours and know that, as with extreme graciousness, the pen of forgiveness has been drawn through the offences of your father and the doors of favour and pardon have been thrown open to his loyalty and devotion; now is the time for you to come to my presence along with your father and your clansmen, for the purpose of saluting the Emperor's threshold, so that after attaining to that happiness you may be exalted among your peers by the grant of a mansab of five Hazari zat with five thousand Sawar rank and suitable rewards, and your father may have his former mansab in the imperial service restored. Your brethren and clansmen who may come along with you, will be enrolled among the servants of the Emperor. Keep your mind composed in all matters and take to your heart this gracious princely letter which is adorned with the impression of my palm .....written on 14 August 1649."*

There is also another letter from Murad to Shivaji Raje, dated 30 November 1649.

"The petition that you had sent with Raghu pandit has been place before me. You have applied for the post of Deshmukh of paraganas Junnar and Ahmadnagar. Rest assured that when I arrive at the imperial court, your desire will be satisfied. It is proper that you should speedily send your wakil (envoy), So that I can ask him about desires and report them to the Emperor, and thus prevent your delay in the transaction of your business."

At the same time, prince Murad Bakhsh wrote to Shahaji Raje on 31st October 1649, as follows ----

"Be honoured with our boundless princely favours and know that the petition which your son Shivaji Raje had sent to me has passed my eyes. As it professes loyalty and service, it has increased my graciousness to him. He has prayed for the pardoning and release of his father. As I am starting on a journey to the imperial court, I shall report all your prayers and get them granted. But it is the way of true devotion and loyalty that you should send your trusted envoy so that the imperial farman giving you safe assurance and adorned with His Majesty's hand impression may be despatched through him. Sambhaji Raje and your other sons, also, by favour of the Emperor will get their release (form trouble) and be honored with their former mansabs and many kinds of favours........I am sending you a gracious robe."

Shahaji Raje released

After his arrest, the all-merciful Adil Shah then put Shahaji under the charge of Sar - I Sarnaubat Ahmad Khan, and he was promised re-instatement if he agreed to peaceably hand over Kondhana Fort that Shivaji Raje had conquered and the fort at Kundurpi to Adilshahi officials.

Shahaji wrote to his two sons-Sambhaji to restore Bangalore and Shivaji Raje to restore Kondana to the Bijapuri officers. Sambhaji obeyed at once but Shivaji Raje did so grudgingly. Luckily he was counselled by Sonopant Dabir to accept his father's orders.

It is interesting to note the discussion that followed between him and Sonopant Dabir after giving up the fort. The Shivbharat in Ch 16/ 1-42 says (loose translation).

Shivaji Raje: *Were it not for my father, I would not have given up this fort. And no one would have the guts to take it from me by force.*

Sonopant: *A fort is not important. Your father is more important. It is therefore right that you gave up the fort. Because if you have surrendered the fort to release your father it is as though you have not surrendered the fort. This enemy has foolishly equated Kondana and Bangaluru to the Meru parvat of Shahaji Raje. That is not an act to be proud of. (Meru parvat was the highest peak in the Himalayas used by the Gods and Demons to churn the ocean and produce amrit-nector of eternal life using the Wasuki snake as a rope)*

On 16 May 1649, Shahaji Raje was called by Adil Shah for an audience vested with a robe of honour and set free with the restoration of all his estates and dignities. A son and heir had been born to Muhammad Adilshah on 5th May 1649, and this joyous event was diplomatically used as a plea for the "pardon" of Shahaji Raje.

Shahaji Raje realized that *"the thorny shrub of his ill deeds had, by the King's grace, sprouted white flowers. The territories that were in his possession prior to his arrest were restored to him."*

This act of kindness and leniency on the part of the King astonished many in the Bijapur Court, and they speculated, that, *releasing Shahaji Raje* the Wily fox' was like *'Knowingly stepping on a snake's tail, straightening the scorpion's sting, regarding thorns as a heap of flowers or resting with a beehive as one's pillow.'*

In conclusion it is important to note the acrimony between Afzal Khan and the Bhosle family.

a-The elder son Sambhaji was killed during the expedition of Kanakgiri , due to the treacherous role of Afzal Khan.

b-Baji Ghorpade had arrested Shahaji Raje when he was sleeping after a night of merriment. Afzal Khan had taken Shahaji in chains from Gingee to Bijapur.

Shahaji Raje never forgot this insult by Baji Ghorpade and Afzal Khan and wrote to Shivaji Raje urging revenge-*'if you are my true son'*

After Shahaji Raje his two loyal officers Kanhoji Jedhe and Dadaji Lohkare who had been arrested along with him, were also freed and they came to meet Shahaji Raje. An emotional Shahaji Raje said *"you were jailed because of me, your watans are from Maval area. Prince Shivba is in Pune. Your glory is well known in that area. If the Mughals or Adilshahi army attack, be loyal to him. Fight them."*

After making solemn vows and presenting both with robes of honor, Kanhoji Jedhe came to meet Shivaji Raje and Dadaji Lohkare went to his watan at Kari.

CHAPTER THREE

Why Adilshahi decided to attack Shivaji Raje?

We have already previously seen that the territory that Shivaji had brought under his control in the Konkan had been in the possession of the Nizam Shah and was annexed by the Adilshah in conformity with the terms of the treaty of 1636 between himself and the Mughals. After the new treaty of 1657, this region was actually to be delivered to the Mughals. But it was amply clear by now that the Adilshah was not likely to honour the commitment. In any case, Shivaji Raje had by this time captured most of that territory, in spite of which Shivaji Raje sent a written request to Aurangzeb to let him keep it! (Map 1/5)

In keeping with the advice of Aurangzeb, on 16th June 1659, Ali Adilshah wrote to Kanhoji Jedhe,

"Shiva(ji) out of thoughtlessness and evil propensities has startedtroubling the followers of Islam residing in the Province of the Nizamshahi Konkan. He has also plundered them. He has captured many forts in the royal territories. Therefore, we have appointed Afzal Khan Muhammad Shahi as the subadar of that province and have sent him with a formidable army.

"Obey the said Khan, discharge your duties as servant, and defeat and extirpate Shiva(ji). Do not give quarter to Shiva(ji)'s men; kill them wherever they may be or from whatever place they may come and thus manifest your devotion and service to the Court.

"Your loyalty will be recognized by the Court in accordance with the said Khan's report and would earn for you promotion and prosperity.

"You should comply with whatever the above-mentioned Khan would write or tell you about the welfare of the state and the royal policies.
Whoever does not obey the orders of the above-mentioned Khan will have to face severe consequences.

The Jedhe Chronology records Kanhoji Jedhe's reaction after he received the farman:

"Like the other Deshmukhs of Maval, Kanhoji Jedhe received a farman issued by Ali Adilshah. Kanhoji took the farman and went to Rajgad along with his five sons to meet Shivaji Raje. When Kanhoji showed the decree to Shivaji Raje, he said: 'Your neighbours Kedarji and Khandoji Khopade, Deshmukhs of Taraf Utravali, have joined Afzal Khan. If you refuse to comply with the royal order, your watan might come in jeopardy. As your life might be in danger, you too go [to the Khan].'

This was the first turning point of the Pratapgad War.

Who was Afzal Khan

Fig 3 / 1 Afzal Khan

On this Kanhoji Naik said: 'The solemn promise I had made to the Maharaja (Shahji) when he assigned me to your charge remains constant. I place my watan at your feet. My sons and I are ready to sacrifice our lives for you, come what may.' Kanhoji Jedhe said this and took an oath. Shivaji Raje asked him to renounce his watan, by taking up a handful of water and letting it flow to the ground, as a symbolic gesture of renouncement]. Kanhoji did so and renounced his watan. Shivaji Raje said to Kanhoji, 'Your family is at Kari. Take them to

Talegaon.' Kanhoji then asked Dadaji Krishna, who was havaldar at Kalyan, to meet him. Retaining Dadaji's elder son Rakhmaji with him, Kanhoji sent both families - his and Dadaji's - to Talegaon. Kanhoji and Shivaji Raje exchanged solemn oaths. Thereafter, the Bandals, Haibatrao Silimbkar, Pasalkar, Marane, Dhamale, Maral and Dohars were summoned and all of them also took solemn oaths of allegiance and raised a force of infantry."

Aurangzeb set out northwards for Agra on 5 February 1658 for staking his claim to the Mughal throne.

It was then that Adilshah started thinking of subduing Shivaji Raje. He was short of courageous generals who could take on Shivaji Raje .Khavas Khan and Fateh Khan had recently died. Siddi Jauhar had rebelled but as we shall see would play an important role in the battle of Panhalgad. Ballol Khan was occupied else where.

Randaula Khan had been the subhedar of Wai and Afzal Khan had been his assistant. There are letters from Randula Khan which bear the phrase '*by the permission of Afzal Khan* 'which means Afzal Khan had the experience of fighting in these hilly areas. After the death of Randula Khan, his son Rustam e Jamah should have inherited the subhedari of Wai. But he was too young therefore Afzal Khan was temporarily appointed in his place. Afzal Khan wanted to be appointed as the permanent Subhedar of Wai therefore he had no alternative but to prove himself and to do that he had to take on Shivaji Raje after Shivaji Raje captured Jawali.

Adil Shah was also aware that Rustum Jemah was friendly towards Shahaji while Afzal Khan was at loggerheads with the Bhosle family.

So he was the best choice or by default, the only choice to be designated to subdue Shivaji Raje.

Ali Adilshah Appoints Afzal Khan

The Shivbharat says in Ch 17/2-11:

Ali Adilshah addressed Afzal Khan thus, *in the whole army you are our biggest well wisher, a destroyer of brahmins and (Hindu) Gods, a second Kalikal, victorious over descendants of Prabhu Ram, you attacked the Raja of Karnapur with the ferocity of an eagle attacking a snake, demolished the city of Madura and stripped it of its gold, the sea and Lanka serves you.*

Oh Afzal Khan when you walk, all the seven peaks, the seven seas and the seven islands tremble,

Hearing your achievements even the Badshah of Delhi cannot sleep at night,

Inspite of this, it is surprising, that the son of Shahaji troubles me day and night.

And I can see no one mightier than you who can subjugate him.

A delighted Afzal Khan replied *"What the King orders with confidence and love, is the King's doing. The officer is only a namesake. If the King does not order his officer how will he know whether the officer is courageous or not ."*

After the king (Ali Adilshah) presented him with his own dagger he said, *'that (the tree of) the observance of the Muhammadi Faith (Islam) would not bloom without the water of his blood thirsty sword and the thorny bushes of infidelity and polyethism (Hinduism) would not burn without the fire of the enemy consuming sword.'*

In about March 1659, Adilshah appointed Afzal Khan with 10,000 horsemen with orders −

"to fan the flames of anger and melt the balance of Shivaji's life in the crucible of destruction and to trample the harvest of his life under the hooves of horses."

It was thought that between Shivaji Maharaj and Afzal Khan, Shivaji Raje was the underdog.

Yet he cautioned:

"even if that black faced infidel (Shivaji) sent a deceitful letter he the (Khan) must not listen to his false words of flattery and do nothing but fling the fire of death on the harvest of his life and pull down the fort of his life."

Afzal Khan on his part bragged

"Who is this Siva? I will bring him back without even dismounting from my horse!"

Afzal Khan's given name was Abdulla and Afzal Khan was the title given to him by Adilshah.

Afzal Khan was not from an aristocratic family. His father was a cook (bhatari). This inferiority complex made him ruthless, cunning and a back stabber. He was a giant of a man and could take on three to four men single handedly.

Afzal Khan was also a religious zealot who would describe himself thus *'Deendar Butshikan'* (religious and breaker of idols), *'Deendar Kufrashikan'* (religious and killer of Kafirs).

In one stone epigraph, Afzal Khan calls himself *'Katile Mutmarridan va Kafiran sikand e Buniyade Butan'* (Killer of rebels and kafirs and Destructor of Idols).

Afzal Khan's seal boasted-

Fig 3/2

His seal states *"Garharz kunad sipahar Azar Fazal Fuzalava Fazal Afzal Azar mulkivah e tasbih awaz ayad Afzal, Afzal. "*

'If the great heavens desire, it may compare the greatness (piousness) of pious man and the greatness (piousness) of Afzal then from the japmala (rosary) everywhere instead of the sound of Allah Allah will emit the sound Afzal, Afzal.'

Afzal Khan was a successful general

By 1638-40, Afzal Khan rose to be deputy to Randullakhan. In the years 1644-46 he was under Mustapha Khan. During the battles in Karnataka, against Shri Rangarai, descendent of Vijajanagar, at Penukonda and against Kutubshah. He showed explanary courage for which he was elevated to the rank of an Independent General.

It was during this period that he murdered Kasturi Ranga, Palegar of Shira, after calling him for a meeting. Thus along with his millitary prowess he was also known for his treachery

In 1648, he was deputed to escort the imprisoned Shahaji Raje to Bijapur.

Later on i.e. 1652 onwards he had taken part in the battles against Shri Rangarai and eliminating kingdom of Jagdevrai in the present Tamil Nadu.

In 1657, Afzal Khan had nearly cornered and trapped Aurangzeb. Aurangzeb then sent an envoy to Khavas Khan, who pondered on the consequences of killing or imprisoning a Mughal prince and allowed Aurangzeb to go free.

An enraged Afzal Khan took revenge and killed Khavas Khan.

We have already seen that he was responsible for the killing of Sambhaji (Shivaji Raje 's elder brother) by artillery fire during the siege of Kanakgiri.

Afzal Khan was a ruthless administrater.

A letter sent by Afzal Khan on 15th July 1654 sheds light on his ruthlessness. The Mukadanm of Afzalpur had left his post and gone to another village during the sowing season. Afzal Khan reminded the mukadam that he regarded the pleasents as his children (pongade) and that the mukadam should go back to his village and oversee the cultivation. Afzal Khan also assured the mukadam all fairness and absolutely no harassment if he performed his duties well.

However, his next statement is shocking.

Afzal Khan warns the mukadam that-

'if he does not resume his duties, he will hunt him down and cut him to pieces and crush him through an oil mill. Further he promises this gruesome punishment will be not only to the wrong doer but also to the families of all those who give him refuge.'

So great was his terror, that when one of the Habshi sardar was informed that Afzal Khan had been detailed to punish him, he, on his own, presented himself in chains in front of Afzal Khan.

But shockingly, he used the word 'Pongade' (which means friends or dependents) for common ryots.

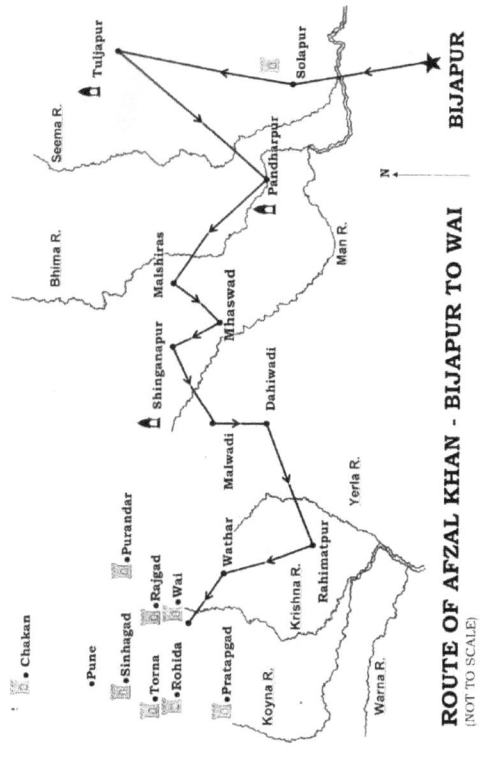

Map 3 / 3

The War Scenario 1659

The politics of the Mughals, the Adilshahi and the Marathas was intermingled and therefore threw up various permutations and combinations.

A MUGHAL -MARATHA COMBINATION

As we have already seen Aurangzeb wanted to capture the Deccan a feat that even his father Shah Jahan or great grandfather Akbar could not achieve.

But Auranzeb was aware that the battle ground of the Deccan was vastly different fron the flat plains of the North. He needed a Deccani partner.

Afzal Khan had already had a skirmish with him, while Shivaji Raje had sent an envoy to him during his coronation. Auranzeb had also reciprocated and sent robes of honour to Shivaji Raje. Therefore Adilshahi was worried that a joint Mughal- Maratha attack would rip apart his kingdom.

It was imperative that Afzal Khan had to subdue Shivaji Maharaj before the Mughal army of Shaista Khan arrived on the scene and like his father Shahaji induce him to join forces with Adilshahi.

That was the only way Adilshah could take on the Mughals.

Therefore Adilshah had ordered Afzal Khan to *"Throw Fire on the life of Shivaji Maharaj, by feigning friendship."*

A MUGHAL - ADILSHAHI ALLIANCE

Shivaji Raje 's worry was the possibility of a Mughal -Adilshahi combination. Shivaji Raje 's strategy was very simple. To defend his territory and destroy Afzal Khan 's Army before the arrival of the Mughals.

Shivaji Raje presumed that there could be an Alliance between the Mughals and Adilshah because though Shivaji Raje had sent a robe of honor, Shivaji Raje was aware of Aurangzeb's letter to Adilshah, where he writes *"Take Shiva out of the Fort. If you wish, give him a Jagir in the south...... I will not take sons of Shahaji or Bahalol Khan into service..."* This clarifies Aurangzeb's assessment of Shivaji Raje and the policy to be adopted towards him.

In July 1659, when Shaista Khan was appointed as the Subhedar of Deccan, he had instructions to subjugate Shivaji Raje. By that time, Afzal Khan had reached Wai. It would have taken six to eight months for Shaista Khan to reach ie by February - March 1660. Then there was the possibility of any of the two armies uniting with the defeat of the third.

Both Shivaji Raje and Afzal Khan were clear in their strategy. Each one wanted to eliminate the other and take on the Mughals.

With the Mughals out of the way, Ali Adilshah decided to deal with Shivaji Raje who had become a thorn in his flesh. In summary, what the Tarikh-i Ali says is as follows:

When the late King [Muhammad Adilshah] fell ill, the banished infidel [Kafir], Shiva (ji) Bhosale, who was the virtual mentor of malevolent Satan in trickery and deceitfulness, plundered the entire province of Konkan and captured the fort of Rahir [Rayri]. When the King died, that malicious infidel [Shivaji Raje] regarded that news as more joyous than the tidings of one's victory and captured [some more] forts in that province [Konkan]. He was extending the hand of repression and injustice like a greedy and hungry dog, that does not feel satisfied with the bone it gets and wants more, and was oppressing the faithful [Muslims]who were engrossed in prayers to God.

Afzal Khan's harem

Before Afzal Khan set out from Bijapur, he spent a month enjoying in his harem. When it was time to go, he had all the 65 ladies of his harem to be drowned in a three storeyed well called Surangbawdi or Khooni Bawdi so that they would not sleep with any other man.

There is an Afzal Makhbara and Masjid at Afzalpura. There was a tradition in Islam to build a tomb before a person's death. Very close to this place now bears titular testimony to the uxoricide: "Sath Kabar".

The burial site of 63 women of Afzal Khan's Harem

Fig 3/ 4

Some say they were pushed into a deep well, while others say that of the 65 wives, 63 unfortunate wives were slain by Afzal Khan. The remaining two got wind of the fate that awaited them, escaped but they were caught by Khan's solders and were killed at different place. Their tomb is seen at different places.

On a platform are 7 rows of graves, all being those of females (a female tomb has flat top). First four rows have eleven graves, fifth row has five graves and sixth and seventh row has seven graves totaling to 63 graves. These have been so regularly placed at equal intervals, and are all so uniform in size and design, that they appear to have been made for persons who had all died at the same time. Just adjacent to the platform is the gallery ie a covered corridor, closed from one end and having arches. At the other end, there is a staircase to go on the roof of this gallery.

Muslims do not have the tradition of "Johar" like Rajputs, so the story of 63 graves of females of the same size and shape in private area of Afzal Khan, become all the more eerie and chilling.

Similarly why different rows have different number of graves is difficult to fathom.

The French traveller Abbe Carre (1672-74) writes *'before Afzul Khan was about to depart (on his mission) he spent a month in merry making with the 62 women in his harem. When the time to quit his harem, his jealousy flamed up with such violence that he could not master it anymore, and it inspired him in the darkest design of which a man is capable. The end was tragic because two at a time over a period of one month, he caused the unfortunate women to be drowned.*

Fig 3/ 5

Cenotaph of Afzal Khan

A cenotaph is a tomb or monument erected in honour of a person or a group of persons whose remains are elsewhere. Thus it is an empty grave.

He named this area Afzalpur. Like Alexander who named 17 Alexandrias after himself, Afzal named three more ie he changed the name of Rahimpur to Afzalpur,

He was called Farzand I Rashid which means 'obedient son' or 'loyal son'.

Departure from Bijapur (April 1659)

In the first week of April 1659, Afzal Khan started from Bijapur. It was essential for him to defeat Shivaji Raje before the advent of the monsoon.

The rainy season starts on 'Mrug Nakshtra', i.e.in 1659 on 24 May and eased by Dashera ie about 15 October. All warfare came to a standstill during this period.

In short Afzal Khan had a window of about a month and a half ie from 1 May to 15 June, to defeat Shivaji Raje.

Afzal Khan's Army

When Afzal Khan left Bijapur his army consisted of about 10,000 infantry and 12,000 cavalry.

Every infantry of 1000 had 12 to16 cannons. The camel guns or mountain guns were 5 to 7 feet long and their bores ranged from 2 to 2.5 inches.

The 80-90 long range cannons were accompanied with about 1000 laborers ie muzzle loaders and breech loaders. There were also 300-400 small range cannons with about 4000 laborers to service this artillery.

There were about 100 elephants, 20 of them were for the royal tents and 80 of them for the long range cannons.

Fig 3/ 6

There were about 1200 camels, 10 percent of these were for small guns while 90 percent for baggage and equipment. These camel guns were called Shuternala, Jejila, Jambur or Garnala. They were about 5 to 6 feet long and could be carried by two men.

Afzal Khan's army also had 46 bullock carts for food, fodder and amunitions.

As we shall see later this total army grew to about 40,000 when he reached Wai.

This was the largest army that had invaded the fledgling kingdom of Shivaji Raje.

Adnyandas says in verse 13 "Compared to the Adilshahi army, Shivaji Raje's army was salt in a lump of dough."

The Preparations by Afzal Khan.

Moving an army of 10,000 infantry and 12,000 cavalry with the attendant artillery was an extremely complicated logistic exercise. Afzal Khan must have utilized about a month for planning and strategy. Besides the man, money and material that he requisitioned, he had with him something unique ie *'Daule'*. These are Blank forms bearing a stamp of Adilshah, and were a sort of power of attorney. Afzal Khan now was the defacto 'Adilshahi' for this campaign. He could give or take away watans, inams, and mansabs.

There were 24 umraos of the Adilshahi who accompanied Afzal Khan. Some of their names are Rustam Zaman, Siddi Halal, Jivaji Devkante, Muse Khan, Baji Ghorpade, Mumbaji Bhosle, Ambar Khan, Yakut Khan, Hasan Khan, Randulla Khan, Ankush Khan, Naikji Kharate, Kalyanji Kharate, Kalyanji Jadhav, Pilaji Mohite, Shankaraji Mohite, Rahim Khan, Pahelwan Khan, Prataprao More.

Each of these Umraos were given definite responsibilities and postings as we shall see later.

The speed of the Mughal Dak was 150 k.m. per day as seen from the fact that 'the treaty of Purander' was signed and sent by Jaisingh to Aurangzeb on Bakri Eid ie 13 June 1665 and it reached Agra on Gulabi Eid ie 23 June 1665. The distance between Pune and Agra is about 1500 km, so one can presume that the speed of dak or government post was about 150 km per 24 hours because the runners /horsemen travelled by night also. The papers called *lakhota* were passed on like a baton in a relay race. Some such Dak arrangement existed in Adilshahi. Most of the vatandars in Shivaji Raje's territory received the Adilshahi farmans by mid-April.

Omens

Starting from Bijapur on an auspicious day and time, Afzal Khan halted at Afzalpura, about three k.m. from the city. Fateh Lashkar was the name of the elephant bearing the standard of Afzal Khan. This elephant died on the first day itself about three km from Bijapur. Adilshah then sent his own elephant as a replacement.

This was the first bad omen.

As if this was not all, legend says that Afzal Khan's Guru Chigni Baba of Thorvegaon saw Afzal's body without the head. This was also a bad omen.

Of course Afzal Khan said *"Go to sleep again and dream again. That head must be the head of Shiva(ji)"*

Afzal Khan's Strategy.

Plan A -Afzal Khan's battle strategy was to lure Shivaji Raje in the plains of Pune and surround him. He knew that the Adilshahi cavalry was far superior to the Maratha cavalry. Plan B- Isolate Shivaji Maharaj in a fort and stop all supplies of food and fodder. Sooner rather than later the Marathas would have to surrender. However he had to do this before the arrival of the Mughals.

Plan C- Negotiate inspite of the instructions of the King 's warning *"that even if that black-faced infidel (Shiva) sent a deceitful letter, he (the Khan) must not listen to his false words of flattery and do nothing but to fling the fire of death on the harvest of his life and pull down the fort of his life.'*

By this time, the Maratha army could match the Adilshahi Infantry but it could not match the 12,000 Cavalry and the Artillary ie 80-90 long range cannons with about 1000 khalasis and 300-400 small range cannons with about 4000 khalasis.to service this artillery.

Afzal Khan's Tortuous Route

Afzal Khan did not go from Bijapur to Pune *as the crow flies*. Instead of going north west, he went eastwards to Pandharpur.

According to the Marathi Ballads and Bakhars, Afzal Khan had ransacked and desecrated temples at Pandharpur, Tuljapur, Kolhapur, Ravalnath, and destroyed the idols there. This was in keeping of his titles of Dindar Butshikan and Dindar Kufrashikan.

Legend says that at Tuljapur he entered the sanctum sanctorum and stood in front of the goddess. He laughed aloud and then challenged Her :

"Ay But – e- kafran! Batao Teri Karamat !" Show me your Prowess.

So saying he desecrated the idol of Tuljabhawani.

Sabhasad says that the idol was broken into pieces, thrown into a handmill and grounded into dust.

Adnyandas in verse 10 says very much the same.

The Bajaji Nimbalkar Episode

War is an expensive business, especially when fought in the Adishahi or Mughal style. Afzal Khan' s 10,000 cavalry cost him two and a half lakhs every month in troopers pay and fodder allowance. As with all Muslim invaders, Afzal Khan decided to make war pay for war. All Hindu temples were a store house of immense wealth. They were also surrounded by residences of affluent merchants and rich bankers. After ransacking Pandharpur, Afzal Khan went to Malavadi. Encamped at Malwadi, Afzal Khan pursued his policy of frightfulness in the hope of cowing Shivaji into submission. Here he imprisoned Bajaji Nimbalkar, Shivaji Raje 's brother-in-law ie Saibai's brother and accused him of spying for Shivaji Raje. Afzal Khan threatened to have him circumcised and trodden to death by an elephant. This was a direct threat to Shivaji Raje and had the expected effect on Shivaji Raje.

However Shivaji Raje did not react with the foolhardiness that Afzal Khan expected. Instead of acting rashly Shivaji Raje decided to find out which Maratha sardar he could interact with in Afzal Khan s army .Naikji Pandhre was a sardar in the Adilshahi army and he could influence Afzal Khan. Shivaji Raje contacted him and asked him to secure the release of Bajaji Nimbalkar. Accordingly, Naikji Pandhre petitioned Afzal Khan that Bajaji Nimbalkar was innocent and if necessary he, Naikji Pandhre was willing to pay a ransom for his release. He also advised Afzal Khan that circumcising Bajaji Nimbalkar would send a wrong signal in the Maratha sardars in Afzal Khan's army.

Afzal Khan demanded 60,000 hons as ransom money for the release of Bajaji Nimbalkar. Naikji Pandhre mortgaged the Deshmukhi of Phaltan and borrowed the 60,000 hons from two money lenders Babubhai and Babanbhai of Malavadi.

Afzal Khan came to Rahimatpur and finally to Wai.

Thus Afzal Khan added 60,000 Hons to his war kitty but he destroyed the trust of his Hindu mansabdars.

But on a personal note, Shivaji Raje must have been satisfied that he fulfilled the last dying wishes of Saibai.

This was the second turning point of the Pratapgad battle.

The Tarikh-i Ali describes Afzal Khan's invasion of Shivaji Raje 's territory thus:

"Afzal Khan set out according to the order of Ali Adilshah and within a few days he transformed Shivaji Raje 's territory into a riding ground for the horses of the victorious army. . The leaders of the rebels went deaf hearing the thunderous sounds of kettle drums of the warriors on the battlefield. The enemy was blinded by hesitation or apprehension."

The third letter by Afzal Khan addressed to Vithoji Haibatrao, Deshmukh of Taraf Gunjan Maval, reads: *"Krishnaji Bhaskar, havaldar of Wai Pargana, spoke to me about you and praised your work. You are well known for your work and this is the time for service. Therefore, trust me, come to Jawli with your men and follow my orders. Join in the campaign and manifest your goodwill towards the state. You will be promoted as per your wish."*

SWOT Analysis by Shivaji Raje

SWOT Analysis equals analysis of strength, weakness, opportunities and threats.

Shivaji Maharaj knew his strength was his mawla infantry and the rocky Sahyadry.

His weakness was the absence of a strong cavalry.

Afzal Khan was both an opportunity and a threat.

Afzal Khan was definitely a threat but, it also was an opportunity for Shivaji Raje to somehow defeat Afzal Khan.

As we saw Afzal Khan reached Pandharpur area by early May.

By mid May, Afzal Khan's army had turned west wards and occupied Pune, Saswad, Supe and Shirval. Shivaji Raje had established his defense line as Chakan-Sinhgad-Purandhar-Rohida. Afzal Khan was at Wai. Even before the arrival of Afzal Khan, Shivaji Raje had started building his line of defense.

In a letter of 12 May 1659, Shivaji Raje had ordered Baji Prabhu Deshpande about establishing a post at deserted Kaslotgad, renaming it as Mohangad. This proves the fact that the work on Wai as the base had started even before 12 May 1659.

"Time for Space."

Shivaji Raje's reaction to Afzal Khan's invasion of Indapur, Baramati, Supe, Sandas, Chakan and Pune area was to retreat from these areas.

Shivaji Raje established Chakan-Sinhgad-Purandar-Rohida as his 'Defense' line

Afzal Khan might have felt that, exploiting the temples at Pandharpur etc. and threatening Bajaji Nimbalkar for conversion and collecting ransom, might provoke Shivaji Raje to attack him at these places. And once Shivaji Raje was in the plain area, Afzal Khan with his superior artillery could easily move to flank, maneuver and destroy Shivaji Raje.

However Shivaji Raje did not even resist, leave aside attacking Afzal Khan's weak force kept in that area and Afzal Khan's plan did not materialise. Shivaji Raje's action of evacuating the land was strategy gaining "Time for Space." By that time the rainy season had set in, movement of the troops were hampered, and Shivaji Raje gained four months respite.

Afzal Khan makes Wai his base.

On 24 May 1659, Afzal Khan reached Wai, which was a pargana place.
Afzal Khan arranged for the living quarters and storage space for his supplies and arms, ammunition for his army. He had brought with him three years' provisions. He also had a huge treasury brought from Bijapur and supplemented it by ransom and loot obtained from Pandharpur, Tuljapur and from Bajaji Nimbalkar.

The situation in June 1659.

1-On 5 June 1659, Aurangzeb sent a robe of honor to Shivaji Raje.

2- By now all the twelve Maval Deshmukhs had received the Adilshahi farmans. This must have caused a great churning .

3-Afzal Khan had by now arrived at Wai.

4-The Pune province was already lost due to the retreat strategy of Shivaji Raje.

5-Khandoji and Kedarji Khopade of Utroli went over to Afzal Khan.

6- After arriving at Wai, Afzal Khan had started recruiting Mavales. The number of recruits is given differently, which ranges from 500 to 5,000. We can consider the figure to be 3,000. Kedarji Khopade was made in-charge of this contingent. It is sure some of the recruits were spies of Shivaji Raje.

Kanhoji Jedhe.

We have already seen that Shahaji Raje's two loyal officers Kanhoji Jedhe and Dadaji Lohkare were imprisoned along with Shahaji Raje from 25 July 1648 to 16 May 1649.All three had sworn revenge and bided their time.

It is at this stage (June 1659) that, Kanhoji Jedhe with his sons came to meet Shivaji Raje at Rajgad, along with the Adilshahi firman and 'poured water on vatan' (relinquished his Vatan to Shivaji Raje). But the actions of Kanhoji Jedhe were for a cause ie Maharashtra Dharma and for loyalty. This electrified the country. There were no more defections. All other Vatandars: Bandal, Pasalkar, Shilimbkar, Marne, Dhamale, Maral, Dohar remained loyal to Shivaji Raje. There would be no more fear of internal dissention. This was most unexpected for Afzal Khan. This news must have spread like wild fire in Adilshahi and the Marathas. This definitely raised the Maratha morale.

This was the third turning point in the Battle of Pratapgad.

Stalemate and Afzal Khan's change of Strategy.

Afzal Khan's plan was to desecrate the Hindu temples of Pandharpur and Tulzapur and enrage Shivaji Raje enough to fight in the open plain.

But Shivaji Raje moved the '*theatre of war*' from Pune to Pratapgad. Afzal Khan's cavalry was not of any use in this hilly terrain especially in the rainy season.

The artillery would become a liability instead of an asset. Ammunition could not be kept dry because of the weather. Afzal Khan's forces in Konkan had to halt. Now Afzal Khan had to engage the Marathas fort by fort, which meant spending five to six months at each fort. It was also not possible to defeat Shivaji Raje before the arrival of the Mughals. Saswad and Shirval catapulted but Purandar defied all attempts of subjugation. All the vatandars of the Bara Mavals were now rock solid in their support of Shivaji Raje.

Afzal Khan reached a stalemate, and he had no option but to use the third part of his strategy ie negotiate. He had to lure Shivaji Raje out of his lair, then seize and kill him.

CHAPTER FOUR

Shivaji Raje's strategic retreat to Jawli.

Shivaji Maharaj went to Jawli on 11 July 1659, that is, he went to Jawli at the height of the rainy season. His wife Saibai was ill at Rajgad.

On 21 July 1659, Aurangzeb was crowned as Emperor at Delhi. Shivaji Raje's envoy, Sonopant was present at the coronation. As per the diplomacy of those times on 30 August 1659, Aurangzeb sent a Khilat for Shivaji Raje. The news must have baffled both Adilshah and Afzal Khan. This *X factor* of the Mughals played an interesting role in the battle of Pratapgad as we shall see.

Shivaji Maharaj divided his forces into two parts. (Map 3/3)

One part was placed under Jijabai at Rajgad with forts like Chakan, Sinhgad, Purandar, Rohida, Torna, Rajgad, Lohagad as its defense line.

As stated earlier in May 1659, Baji Prabhu was ordered to establish Mohangad. Shivaji Raje 's defense line ran as Rohida - Kenjalgad - Kamalgad - Mahabaleshwar - Makarandgad - Mahipatgad - Palgad – Songad- Raigad.

Pratapgad was the Headquarter of this force.

The Maratha troops were as follows: 1,000 in 15 major forts ie 15,000

Javli- Pratapgad, Konkan Mahad Rajgad had 10,000 each ie 50,000

Thus the total infantry was 65000 The Cavalry under Netoji was10,000.

Afzal Khan wins the fist round.

Afzal Khan had an army as follows Janjira Siddi 8,000, Pune Area 5,500,

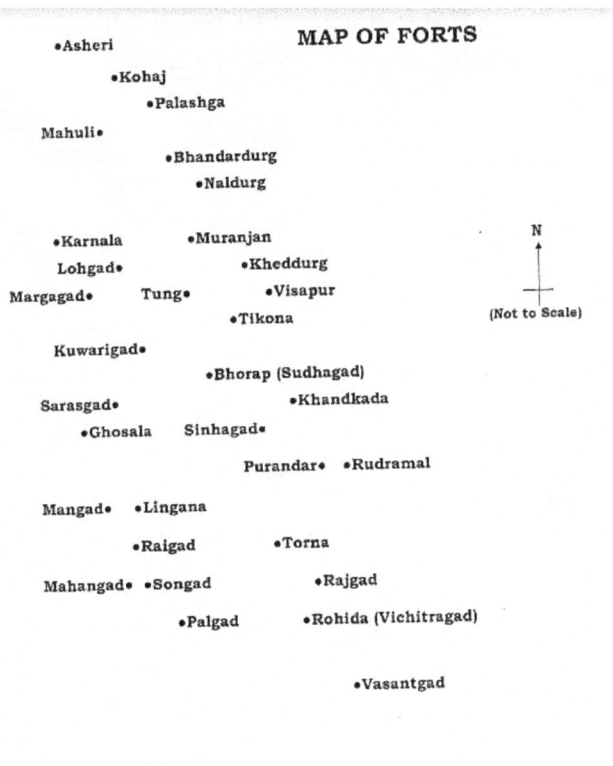

Map 4/1

Sarvarkhan 5,000, Dabhol 6,000 and Wai 16,000 ie Total 40,500 Of these, the main Cavalry of 10,000-12,000 was at Wai and 3000-4000 at Pune area. Most of the artillery would be at Wai. Afzal Khan might not have heavy guns, when he came to Pratapgad, but would have siege guns, Sutarnala (Camel artillery), Rockets and Bandookchis.

In April-May 1659 Afzal Khan had concentrated his troops in Pune and Pandharpur anticipating that Shivaji Raje would attack there. But Shivaji Raje remained at Rajgad. Also Jijabai, Saibai, child Sambhaji and Council of Ministers were at Rajgad. That time the Theatre of War was in the North i.e. Rajgad.

But this theater of War shifted to the South of the river Neera when Shivaji Raje went to Jawli.

As can be seen from the Map 1/4 Afzal Khan had conquered the flat lands like Indapur, Baramati, Supe, Sandas, Chakan and Pune.

Only Rajgad, Sinhgad, Mahabaleshwar, Pratapgad, Poladpur area remained under the control of Shivaji Raje.

Afzal Khan had practically achieved his first mission.

'Defence in Depth' Strategy of Shivaji Raje

Shivaji Raje was adopting a 'Defence in Depth' Strategy. Shivaji Raje 's strategy was

1. Make all the major forts invincible by keeping the required supplies and men.
2. Full defense line of border forts, with small defended posts in between.

Because of the rainy season, the progress of both sides had come to a standstill.

Afzal Khan had realised that Shivaji Raje could not be subdued without fighting, and Shivaji Raje also realised that he could not drive away Afzal Khan.

And interestingly both were unable to predict the outcome of the X factor ie *the Mughals*. Both wanted a result before the Mughals could arrive.

Morale of Afzal Khan's Troops

From May to August 1659, the morale of Afzal Khan's Troops oscillated from high to low.

In the first few months Afzal Khan's army had a free run of the land as there was no confrontation from the Marathas.

Afzal Khan had collected Rs 60,000 from Bajaji Nimbalkar. This might have raised the morale of the Muslim troops, but certainly lowered that of the Hindu troops.

Afzal Khan 's army had to camp in the open in the rainy season. All soldiers suffer in such cases. They get wet, the oxen get wet and most important the gun powder is liable to get wet.

At the same time, they could not forget the two omens.

.1- Afzal Khan's elephant had died.

2- Afzal Khan's Guru had seen his body without his head.

Every passing day had a demoralizing effect on the Adilshahi army.

Morale of Shivaji Raje's troops.

The Morale of Shivaji Raje's troops oscillated from low to high.

1-After receiving the threatening farmans of Adilshah only three watandars went over to Afzal Khan. The tide turned after all other watandars followed Kanhoji Jedhe who vowed loyalty by offering to relinquish his watan. Kanhoji Jedhe lived up to the promise that he had given to Shahaji Raje.

In Shirval pargana three brothers had made an affidavit stating *"Any loss caused because of siding with Shivaji Maharaj will be shared equally among the three."*

2- Shivaji Raje had an *'Oracle from Goddess'*. Legend says that Shivaji Raje's sleep was broken by the vision of Godess Bhavani who urged him to confront Afzal Khan boldly and promised him victory and her full protection.

The Shivbharat in Ch 20 /2-8 says :

Shivaji Raje saw before him Varda – vishamata like a new idea. She was wearing jewellery of diamonds, her feet were adorned with alta (red dye) her lustre was like the champa flower, she was draped in sky blue clothes and looked vey young.

Her face shone like the full moon, she had a smile like the blue lotus, her lips like the new coral, her forehead glowed with a tilak, her ears shone with ornaments,

from her nose hung a nose stud, her arms were slim, she had a lotus in her hand and gracefulness in her fingers.

Her whole body was shining with diamonds, from her neck hung layers of garlands of jewels, the garland reached up to her umbilicus, her black blouse was embedded with golden flowers, she had a diamond studded waist band.

At first the morale was low and the Watandars shrank from the idea of resistance to Afzal Khan. This was their first encounter with a regular force of Bijapur. Tales of Afzal Khan's cruelty, physical prowess, ruthlessness, battle strategy and tactics had preceded him. At the first council of war the watandars urged Shivaji Raje to make peace as they feared the enemy was too strong and hostilities would cause a great loss of life to their side. But Shivaji Raje reasoned that Afzal Khan would kill him as he killed Sambhaji (his elder brother) at Kanakgiri. He decided he would rather die fighting, than become a vassal.

Sabhasad says "When he learnt this, the Raja decided to mobilise all his forces, fight at Jawli and to go to Pratapgad in person. Then he was dissuaded by all; "You (they counselled) should not give battle; peace should be concluded."

The Raja answered to that - "As he killed Sambhaji, so will he kill me. I will do what is possible before I am killed. Peace I will not conclude."

This decision was made. That night Sri Bhavani of Tuljapur appeared (to him) in a bodily shape and said - "I am pleased. I shall assist you in everything. At your hands I shall get Afzal killed. I grant you success. Thou should have no anxiety."

In this manner did the goddess enliven him with resolution and confidence and assured him of security. The Raje awoke, called Jija Bai Au and related to her the details of the dream.

Sabhasad further says that : When the the Sri had said so, the Raje regained consciousness. The *karkun* (clerk) who was with (the Raje), had put the Goddess 's speech into writing, (then) informed the Raje of it. Then the Raja said - "The conclusion of peace will also cause loss of life. If we fight and win, well and good, if life is lost fame remains. A verse runs to this effect- "Victory brings fortune, death the celestial maids; This body is but transient, What terror has then death in battle?"

If I kill Afzal Khan and win victory, then I shall remain what I am. If perchance I lose my life in the course of the war, then there is Sambhaji Raje, deliver the kingdom to him and place yourselves at his commands."

This was the fourth turning point and the Marathas decided to fight.

4- Role of climate and terrain in war.

It is said that in the wars between Russia and Napoleon it was General Winter rather than the Russian army that defeated Napoleon.

It was the same with Hitler when he invaded Russia during the second World War.

In the case of the Deccan it was General Sahyadri that the enemy had to taken on. Sahyadri as we discussed earlier meant tall lofty peaks, dense forests and incessant torrential rains.

By the time Afzal Khan came to Wai, the rainy season had started, Shivaji Raje's troops were sheltered in the forts, fortresses, gadhis or wadis while Afzal Khan's army was lodged in tents. No fragile cloth tent can give solid protection of a stone wall. At the height of the rainy season, when the Theatre of War shifted to the south, Shivaji Raje came to the dreaded area of Jawli. This also raised the morale of his troops.

As the following Fig 4/2 shows the temperature also dropped in the evening.

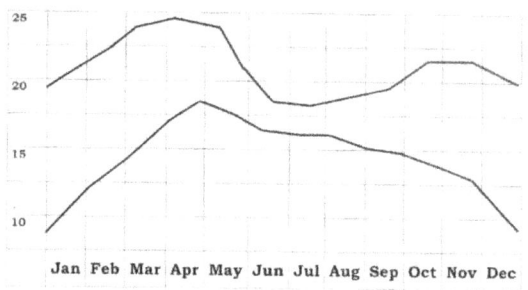

TO SHOW TEMPERATURE IN PRATAPGAD

Fig 4/2

To show how confident the Marathas were we have to fast forward to 1663 Shivaji Raje later wrote to Aurangzeb "even the steed of imaginable exertion is too weak to gallop over this hard country and that its conquest is difficult. My home is unlike the forts of Kalyani and Bidar and is not situated on spacious plain .It has lofty mountain ranges and abysmal valleys."

Shivaji Raje was therefore on a higher and stronger ground. This had a definite effect on the course of war in the future. The Mughals had started from Agra but, were yet to arrive. Both Afzal Khan and Shivaji Raje were closely watching their approach, and both wanted the Mughals to be as late as possible.

In the circumstances, both sides could not afford the stalemate and therefore the war of negotiations started.

AUGUST 1659

Aurangzeb's Firman -the X factor

Aurangzeb was coronated on 06 Jun 1659.

On 14th July 1659, he sent a firman to Shivaji Raje stating "......*am sending Shaista Khan, act according to his advice.....*" Aurangzeb also sent a Khillat (Robe of Honour), along with the firman and it must have reached Shivaji Raje by 15 August 1659. Afzal Khan also must have come to know of this development.

It was therefore very clear that, the chances of Shivaji Raje aligning with the Mughals was greater. So it was imperative for Afzal Khan to kill or imprison Shivaji Raje before the arrival of Shaista Khan in the Deccan. By any means: fight or negotiations.

This was the fifth turning point in the battle of Pratapgad.

SEPTEMBER 1659

The Reasons for Negotiations

On 5 September 1659 Saibai, the first wife of Shivaji Raje died. This was the height of the monsoon.

After a decent period of mourning the war winds must have started blowing.

All generals wish to conquer their enemies through peaceful negotiation rather than a long drawn bloody and costly war.

Afzal Khan was no different, but his reasons for negotiations were as follows:

1. His troops were halted because of the rains.

2. As Afzal Khan's plans of luring Shivaji Raje in the open failed, Afzal Khan had to enter into a long drawn campaign and fight Shivaji Raje fort by fort.

3. Shivaji Raje might join Shaista Khan who had set out from Aurangabad on 28 January 1660.

Shivaji Raje's reasons for negotiations were as follows:

1. Afzal Khan could not be defeated.

2. After the arrival of Shaista Khan, the Mughal war machine could afford long sieges. They could starve the garrisons fort by fort. After sometime Shivaji Raje would have no option but to surrender and then face death or; to be pushed into the ignominy of the south like his father Shahaji.

3. The Mughals were a mighty force, so if Shivaji Raje could have a treaty with Afzal Khan, both could fight together with the Mughals. Afzal Khan would also vacate his country.

It was in this stalemate, Afzal Khan and Shivaji Raje entered into negotiations without revealing their intentions.

Shivaji Raje's spies

Shivaji Raje's spymaster Vishvasrao Nanaji Dighe used to visit Afzal Khan's camp in disguise of Mari Aai (Disciple of Godess) and used to get information. So Shivaji Raje was well aware about the morale of the troops, troop strength, movements, supplies of food, fodder and ammunitions etc.

We are sure that Afzal Khan also had his spies, but as we shall see Shivaji Raje was able to convince Afzal Khan there was an atmosphere of fear and anxiety in the Maratha camp.

October 1659

Afzal Khan sent the Envoy first.

On 5 September Saibai died at Rajgad and Shivaji Raje must have been with her till the end.

By 20 September, Shivaji Raje must completed all the rituals at Rajgad.

After that he must have moved to Pratapgad.

At the time of taking leave of his mother, Jijamata had warned "*Shivba, budhine kam ghe Sambhaji che usne ghe*"(Child Shivba .Be alert .Take revenge for your elder brother Sambhaji.)

That year Diwali was on 7th October and 8 October was Eid.

On 10 October, Afzal Khan sent Krishnaji Bhaskar as his envoy to Pratapgad.

Afzal Khan was a general famous for his brutal style of warfare.

So it was surprising that instead of sending his rampaging and ravaging army, he had sent a docile envoy.

Shivaji Raje was known to be an excellent and magnanimous host. He must have welcomed the envoys with costly gifts and robes of honor.

Shivaji Raje sent Pantaji Gopinath as his envoy.

Pantaji Gopinath was a brahmin from Hivre who was the Deshkulkarni of Supe and Baramati parganas. In 1547, he was the Muzumdar of Pune. From 1656 he was the chitnis of Shivaji Raje. Pantaji Gopinath was part of the inner circle of Shivaji Raje and absolutely trustworthy. He used to play *sagargotya* with Jijamata and everyone called him uncle. This was the person that Shivaji Raje selected to represent him as an envoy to Afzal Khan.

Legend says Pantaji Gopinath was one of retainers that Jijamata brought along with her, when she married Shahaji.

(Sagargotya is a game of dice played with the seeds of Caesalpinia Bonduc.)

Afzal Khan 's envoy Krishnaji Bhaskar.

Krishnaji was first deputed to meet the Marathas who would cross over to Afzal Khan.

On about 11 October, Krishnaji Bhaskar met Shivaji Raje at Pratapgad. A deliberate atmosphere was created to show that Shivaji Raje and the Marathas were absolutely terrified.

The Shivbharat Ch 18/55-65 says that Krishnaji Bhaskar met Shivaji Raje in the last week of October 1659 and presented Afzal Khan 's pompous and aggressive letter –

"Your frequent insolence these days is causing much anguish to the Adilshah. You have brought into your possession that territory replete with hill-forts which had been won by the Adilshah after the dissolution of the Nizamshahi, and which he had ceded to the Mughals with the desire to sue for peace. Because of your constant good fortune, you have captured at every possible opportunity more and more of the territory belonging to the ruler of Rajpuri, because of which he has been encircled and is infuriated. You invaded and captured by force the invincible and extensive kingdom of the Chandrarao. You conquered Kalyan and Bhiwandi and demolished the mosques there. Muslims are still angry with you as you have thoroughly plundered and humiliated them. Taking no cognizance of your own strength, you have imprisoned Muslim priests and dared audaciously to block the path of Islam. You blatantly brandish the trappings of an Emperor: sit without authority upon a golden throne; bestow rewards or mete out punishments to people; you have willfully stopped paying obeisance to those deserving respect since you have become independent. You have grown incorrigible and are not afraid of lesser persons (compared to me, i.e. Afzal Khan]. Therefore, the triumphant Adilshah has sent me (against you]. "An army of six kinds [of troops] sent under my command by orders of the Adilshah, has been persuading me to open hostilities against you without further delay. Muse Khan

and others, who are eager to fight against you and desire to conquer Jawli, have been encouraging me to wage war. Therefore, obey my orders, conclude a treaty and surrender all your forts and provinces to me. You should hand over the strong forts like Sinhgad and Lohgad, Prabalgad, Purandar, the Chakan town and the territory between the Bhima and Nira rivers to the powerful Emperor of Delhi and surrender yourself to him. Ali Adilshah demands Jawli, which you have seized from Chandrarao."

The tone of this letter was very contemptuous and showed that Afzal Khan regarded only Shivaji Raje as an upstart rebel whom he had come to discipline.

The next day when Krishnaji Bhaskar came to the court, Shivaji Raje said in all innocence,

"I respect Afzal khan as much I respect my father Shahaji Raje. I will meet my uncle. I have no doubts in my mind Khan saheb has my well being at heart. I will definitely heed his advice."

As Shivaji Raje accepted the proposal to meet Afzal Khan, all that remained was to determine a meeting place. Afzal Khan wanted to meet at Wai and Shivaji Raje wanted the meeting at the foot of Pratapgad Fort.

As we saw, Shivaji Raje appointed Pantaji Gopinath as his envoy.

Shivaji Raje was meek and beseeching in his reply to Afzal Khan.

The Shivbharat Ch 19/1-10 says:

"It is gracious of you, who subdued in battle all the chieftains of Karnataka, to show me at least this much compassion. You are incomparably powerful. You are a man of great strength. Your existence has embellished the earth and you are not deceitful in the least. Come to Jawli in order to drink in the scenic beauty of the woods. I feel at this juncture that it would be appropriate for you. to come to Jawli. Your visit will dispel my fear and, more over, it will add to my prestige. I feel that, but for one as valorous as you, neither the forces of the arrogant Mughals nor those of the Adilshah are worth anything. Proceed cautiously towards Jawli. I will hand over Jawli and the forts you have demanded to you. It is difficult even to look you in the eye, but after seeing you I will place my

sword before you without any doubt or misgiving. Your soldiers will experience pleasures of the nether world (patal) in this vast and pristine forest."

Krishnaji Bhaskar and Pantaji Gopinath reached Wai with the reply given by Shivaji Raje. Pantaji Gopinath was surprised at the changed scenario at Wai. From a pargana place it had changed into a city of tents.

Afzal Khan, like all other Mughal and Adilshahi generals had with him two sets of field tents each carried by elephants. When he set out from the first, the other was fitted at the place where he would stop that day. Each set of tents contained houses for him and next to it was the tent in which he used to give an audience. This was followed by bed chambers, private rooms, gardens full of fruits and flowers, conveyed in millions of vases and so delicious that one who saw them would doubt whether they were naturally grown.

Krishnaji Bhaskar returned to Wai and he advised Afzal Khan that with the right precautions, it was safe to meet Shivaji Raje below Pratapgad.

The Jedhe Chronology has the following entry under Shaka 1581:

"Afzal Khan sent his envoy Krishnaji to Pratapgad to meet Shivaji Raje in the month of Kartik (7 October to 4 November 1659). Shivaji Raje gave him robes of honor and sent him back with the decision that the interview (between Afzal Khan and Shivaji Raje) would be held below the Pratapgad fort."

As per Sabhasad Bakhar, '*Pantaji Gopinath asked for 'Kriya' (solemn pledge of safety) from Afzal Khan and Afzal Khan did give the pledge. In turn Afzal Khan also asked for a pledge from Shivaji Raje. As instructed, Pantaji gave the pledge. After that the meeting near Pratapgad was confirmed."*

Krishnaji Bhaskar had done a laudable job. He was asked to set up a meeting and he had done what was expected of him for which Afzal Khan must have commended him.

Adnyandas says in his powada *"On hearing that Shivaji Raje was willing to meet him, he started swaying like a cobra dancing to the been."*

Krishnaji Bhaskar convinced Afzal Khan that a meeting with Shivaji Raje at Pratapgad was not dangerous.

This was the Sixth turning point in the Pratapgad battle.

Why did Afzal Khan decide on a meeting?

The reasons why Afzal Khan sent an envoy to Shivaji Raje proposing a meeting was,

1. The campaign would have lasted for three years if no meeting was held.

2. The Mughals were on their way and they could partner with Shivaji Raje. The intelligence gained during the visit of Krishnaji to Pratapgad must have convinced Afzal Khan that Shivaji Raje was scared to the bone by his name alone, and could be easily convinced. Possibly Afzal Khan was also convinced that Shivaji Raje's advisers were also alarmed and wanted a treaty rather than a bloody war.

However, Afzal Khan's advisors were aghast at the prospect of going to the dense forest of Jawli. They tried to dissuade him from entering this lion's den.

Shivbharat says in Ch19 /25-35

"Khawind if Shivaji Raje completely trusts you and wishes to surrender to you all his kingdom, why does he insist on you going to Jawli ? why does he not come here to Wai and pay his (mujra) respects."

They argued that since he was coaxing the Khan to go there, he must have thought up some daring plan and that the hilly and thickly wooded terrain was unsuitable for deployment of cavalry.

However, Afzal Khan did not listen to them. Ironically he made up excuses for Shivaji Raje.

Shivbharat Ch 19 /41-44 says *"An enemy who is himself proud and has been consistently committing crimes will not come to me on his own."*

You are praising him because you do not understand my achievements. The hoofs of my galloping horses have destroyed the army of the kings of Karnataka. I have destroyed many cities and destroyed all idols. I, who is the best of all (warriors) and am angry. Even if yamadoot were to know that I have come near him, he will make a plea for a treaty (surrender)."

But by now the waiting must have made Afzal Khan impatient. He was obsessed with the idea of *confronting that Siva and squeezing the life out of him.*

The Shivabharat Ch 19/30 says *the Khan, "deciding to go to Jawli, told the officers in his army that the move would not be fraught with any great risk as they had well equipped and vigilant soldiers."*

A Dutch letter dated 5 May 1660, sent from Vengurle, too, says his advisers tried *"to persuade him away from his decision but that the vainglorious Khan punished them - the nose of one was cut off, another was spitted (placed upon a sharpened stake so that the victim's weight drove the stake up his entrails), but that the third being Rustam-i Zaman's brother, got off with only a rebuke."*

Shivaji Raje had thrown the gauntlet and the proud Afzal Khan had no optional but to pick it up. He is said to have boasted *"Although not born in a high family like Rustum Jemah, I abide by the code of nobility."*

Afzal Khan had never tasted failure. His ruthlessness and cunning was matched by none so far. In the process he had developed a megalomania. Such a man feels he is the chosen one of God, if not God himself. And he does not accept advice.

As the field of action was unfavorable for artillery action, Afzal Khan left his heavy luggage and treasury at Wai and started towards Jawli with the remaining force.

Out of the army of 40,000 that Afzal Khan had, he could only field about 15,000.

Shivaji Raje had dictated the field of action and depleted Afzal Khan's effective force.

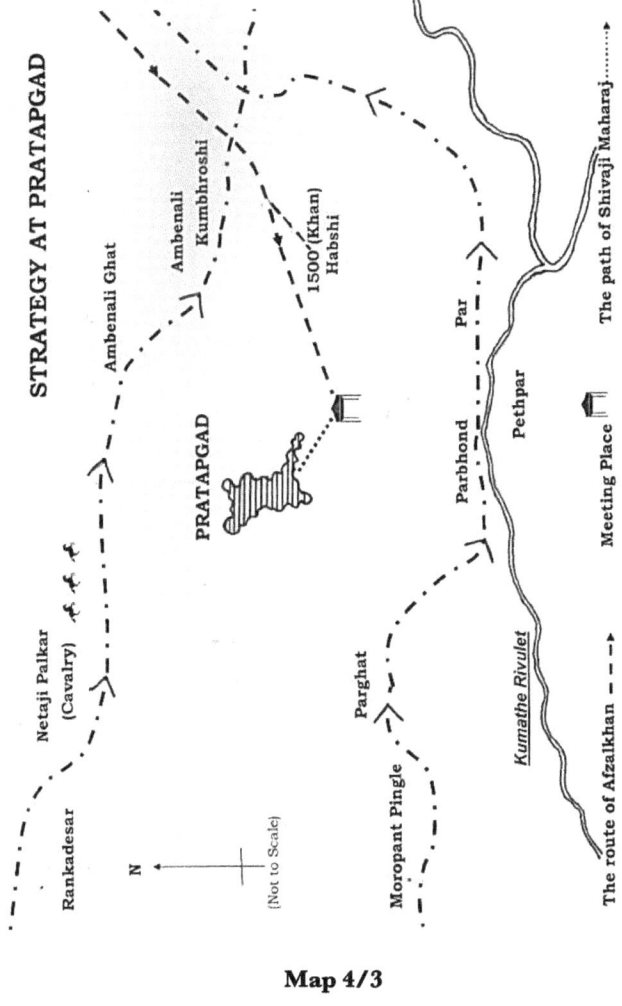

Map 4/3

Shivaji Raje depended on mobility, rapidity and surprise. Shivaji Raje strictly did not have a single elephant, cannon or nautch girl in his army.

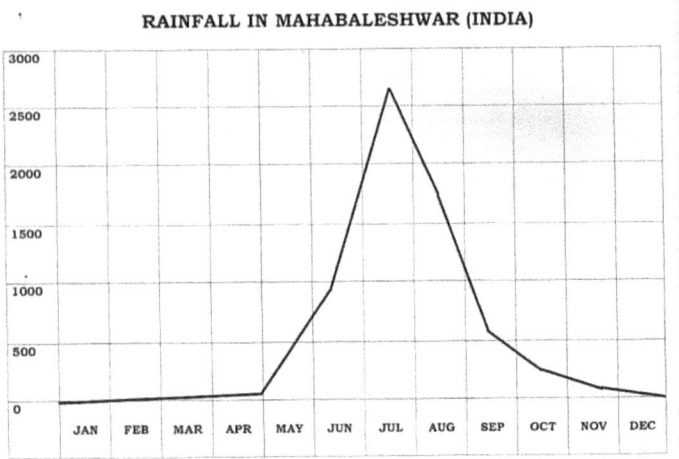

Fig 4/4

Afzal's willingness to come to Pratapgad was the seventh turning point.

Both Krishnaji and Pantaji went to Pratapgad in the second week of October.

As stated earlier, a personal meeting was a must. As per Bakhars and other sources, Krishnaji came to fix a place for the meeting and other modalities. When Krishnaji came back from his first trip, Afzal Khan commended him and said, *"Your fixing a meeting with Raje is very creditable"*.

For Afzal Khan it was very simple. *To kill or imprison Shivaji Raje a personal meeting was necessary. And Krishnaji had done what was expected of him."*

Greedy Traders

It is well known fact that traders (banjaras) of all types and numbering up to 5000 bullock carts, accompanied the armies. Every commodity from grains to cloth to jewelry was available. However we shall restrict ourselves only to jewelry.

After every bout or skirmish, officers who proved their valor were commended and presented with robes of honor, titles, watans and daggers embedded with emeralds and rubies. Such a group of jewelers were a part of the entourage of Afzal Khan.

At this point Pantaji Naik made a request to Afzal Khan that Shivaji Raje wanted to present gifts to all the nobles who had accompanied him. He did not have rubies and emeralds befitting the nobles. So he requested Afzal Khan to allow the traders to accompany him to Pratapgad, where Shivaji Raje could select the precious stones for gifting to the Adilshahi nobles. To Afzal Khan it was a sign of meekness and so he agreed to send the traders.

The Shivabharat Ch 20 /60-63 records:

"The traders showed the precious stones to Shivaji Raje who was eager to buy them. He took all the precious stones from the traders he had invited from Afzal Khan's camp and asked them to stay on the fort. The greedy and foolish traders who had lost their sense of reason owing to their lust for quick profit, failed to realize that they were confined on the mountain top from all sides." Ie virtually in a prison.

The Mughal system of hunting animals

The Mughal tradition of hunting was about bringing out the warrior in an Emperor and his soilders. The hunting method of the Mughals, called 'Qamargah', was like a battle plan. Hundreds of men were employed as, drum beaters, mahouts, security men, assistants and trained elephants known as kumkis. After locating a herd of wild animals to be captured it was encircled by the team of the hunters sealing all routes of escape. Their job was to trap the animal in a circle and lead it to an area encircled by nets or fences. Once trapped, the animal usually a lion was shot by the Emperor, who was seated on an elephant and assisted by trained cheetahs and dogs.

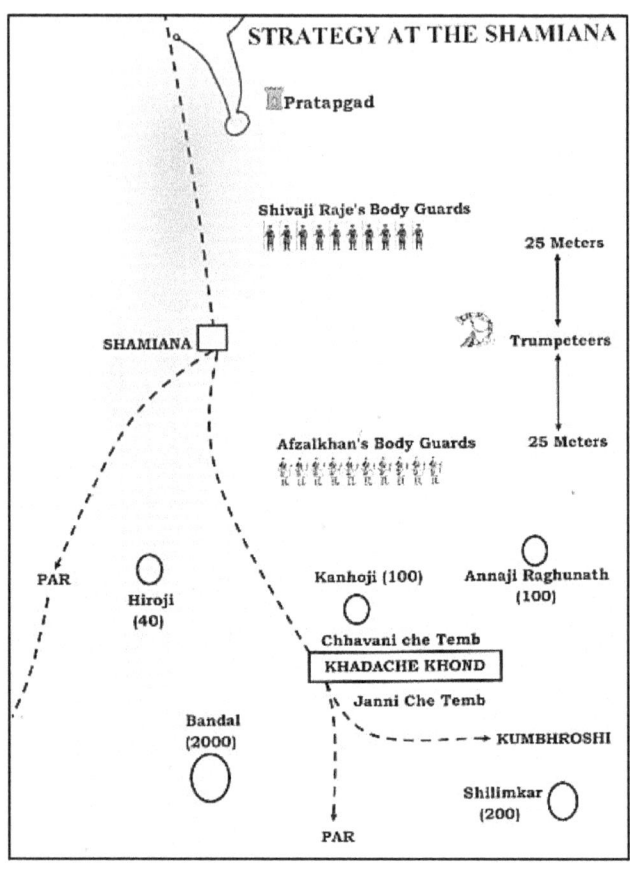

Fig 4/ 6

To prevent animals from going astray, big fires were lit, drums beaten and gun shots fired to scare the animals and keep them confined. Following this activity of keeping the animals within the confined space, building of the enclosure was carried out. This enclosure was located in a camouflaged area along one of the main paths of the animals. The enclosure was fortified with slanting buttresses and ties. A highly secure entrance gate fitted with spikes was built. The entrance path to guide the animals was done through two fences.

Similar hunts must have been organized by Afzal Khan, the difference being that this time Afzal khan was the prey and the Marathas were the hunters.

The Protocol for the Meet

As per the Shivbharat 21/1-8 the Protocol for the meet was as follows (Fig 4/6)

1. The venue was in Shivaji Raje 's territory, so all the logistics was the responsibility of Shivaji Raje ie the setting up the shamiana and the construction of a road from Par to the shamiana.

2. It was agreed that, both Afzal Khan and Shivaji Raje would be armed since neither of them was a victor or vanquished.

3. In the shamiana Afzal Khan would be accompanied by Krishnaji Bhaskar and Shivaji Raje by Pantaji Gopinath. Besides the envoys there would be no other person.

4. Outside the shamiana ten armed bodyguards of both Shivaji Raje and Afzal Khan would then station themselves at a distance of an arrow-shot. (15-20 metres).

Shivbharat Ch 21/1-3 gives names of all the Marathas. They were

Sambhaji Kawji, Kataji Ingle, Kondaji Kank, Yesaji Kank, Krishnaji Gaikwad, Surtaji Kakde, Jiva Mahale, Visaji Murumbak, Sambhaji Karwar, and Siddi Ibrahim.

From Afzal Khan 's side the names we know are Fazal Khan, Muse Khan, Bada Sayyed, Abdul Sayyad, Pahilwan khan, Pilaji and Shankarji Mohite. Both of them were paternal uncles of Saibai ie they were uncle in law of Shivaji Raje.

5. Out of these, two persons from both sides would be just outside the shamiana. Bada Sayyad and one more from Afzal Khan's side and Jiva Mahalya and Sambhaji Kavji from Shivaji Raje's side.

6. At a distance of 300-500 metres, Afzal Khan should bring about a thousand troops. Shivaji Raje would have his troops in the fort.

7. As per protocol, Afzal Khan was elder, so Afzal Khan would go to the shamiana first and Shivaji Raje was to come to meet him there.

This is confirmed by Shivabharat Ch 21/3-8 which says:

"Afzal Khan would go to the meeting place in a palanquin, leaving his force where it is. He would be armed and take with him just two or three servants, reach the place of the meeting on a machi of the Pratapgad fort and await Shivaji Raje's arrival in the pavilion. Shivaji Raje, too, would be armed and would arrive there to welcome and honor the guest according to custom. Ten armed, brave and loyal bodyguards of each party would then place themselves at a distance of an arrow-shot. After the two have met, they would proceed with secret discussions as would bring happiness to all."

While the conditions of the meeting were being tabulated Pantaji visited Wai many times. (Fig 5/1) During this time he talked to many officials of Afzal Khan especially the Hindu sardars who were hurt by the treatment meted out to Baji Nimbalkar at Malwadi. He also gave them bribes to find out what Afzal Khan really had in his mind. Did he want a treaty or was his intention to kill Shivaji Raje or at least imprison him ? After interviewing a few Maratha sardars Pantaji came to the conclusion that Afzal Khan wanted to kill or imprison him. They must have shown him the cage that Afzal Khan had brought with him to take Shivaji Raje to Bijapur locked up like an animal.

It is here that Pantaji assured Shivaji Raje that *"Khan is of evil mind. He plans, to meet you, commit treachery, arrest you and take you to Bijapur.*

Pantaji then put forth a plan -

"If you have the daring I will convince Afzal Khan *to come to Jawli.*

You courageously embrace him and kill him and loot his complete army and baggage. Make this kingdom yours."

Netoji Palkar

During this period, whilst Shivaji Raje was buying time, Netoji Palkar was eager to attack the Bijapuri army. The instructions that Shivaji Raje gave him are described by the Shivabharat in Ch 23/16-17:

"When Shivaji Raje's commander-in-chief, who was renowned, devoted, valiant and as swift as an eagle, heard about the plight to which the country had been reduced by the enemy's army on the orders of Afzal Khan, he returned to Shivaji Raje's happy and contented country with 7,000 cavalry besides infantry, eager to subdue the enemy. He vowed to kill Kharade, Pandhare, Jadhavrao, Siddi Hilal and Saif Khan. When Shivaji Raje learnt about the resolve of his commander, be sent him a message by the hands of his emissary that 'the adamant Muslim demon named Afzal will be coming to Jawli to make peace. Hence, do not start hostilities with his soldiers till negotiations about the treaty are concluded, yet keep yourself fully prepared. You must definitely go to Wai the same day I meet the Khan.' So, Netoji stopped halfway and did not wage war against the enemy."

Afzal Khan's Camp

It is possible that at first Afzal Khan must have refused to go to Jawli and insisted on an interview at Wai. It goes to the credit of Pantaji Gopinath that he could convey the dread and fear that Shivaji Raje was supposed to feel.

Most important Pantaji insisted that the meeting was possible if and only if Afzal Khan came to Jawli as Shivaji Raje was terrified. After the meeting *Afzal khan was free to take* Shivaji Raje *wherever he wanted.'*

Pantaji further urged that Afzal Khan was free to come with his huge army so what was the worry ? This was a direct affront to Afzal Khan's ego. And Afzal khan fell into this trap.

Pantaji had done his job. Shivaji Raje paid him 5000 hons.

(one hon is about three gms of gold).

Any negotiation is a strategic discussion that resolves an issue in a way that both parties find acceptable.

Afzal Khan marches to Jawli

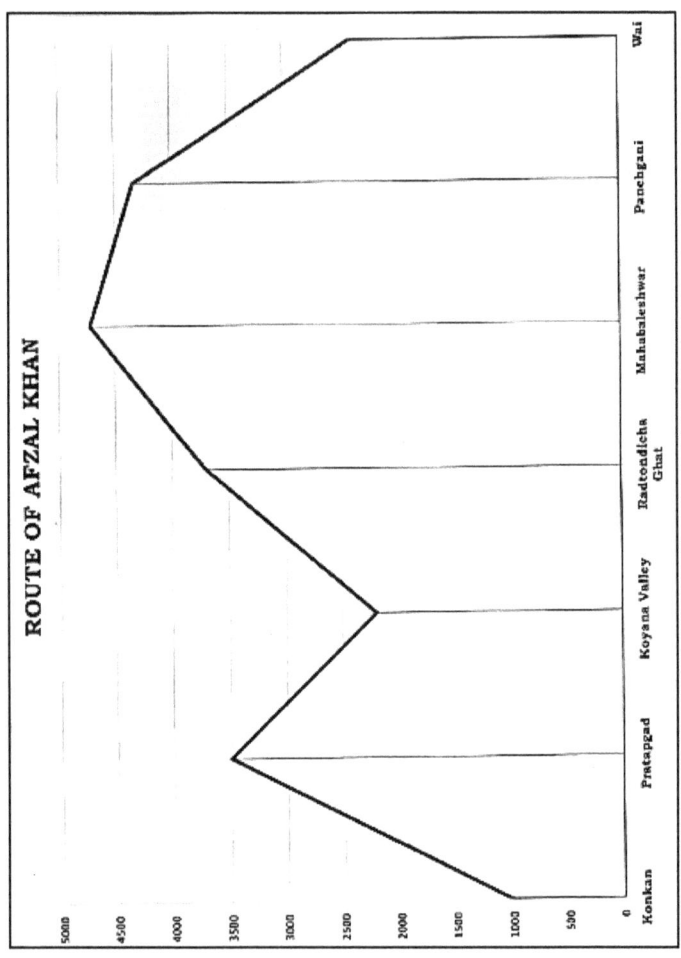

Fig 4/5

Afzal Khan had started from Wai around 1st November and along with his troops reached Koyana valley around 6th November at

Peth Par ie a distance of 35 km. The heavy guns were left behind at Wai with due security. Small guns (sutarnala) and rockets must have been carried on elephant and camel's back, leading them by reins. As seen in the Map 4/5 he camped at Kusgaon, Chikhli, Taighat, Gureghar, Lingmala, Dare Haroshi and Dudhoshi This involved a three km ascend at Pasarni ghat to Chikhli followed by a sixteen km trek though dense jungle and then again a three km steep descent to Par by Radtondi ghat. The Shivbharat says that Afzal Khan's army when reached the peak of a hill it saw the heavens, while when it descended into a deep valley it was an abyss.

The route was steep and slippery with ups and downs, zigzags, sharp hairpin bends, precipitous cliffs and vertical rock faces. Even these roads were washed away by waterfalls that interrupt the rivers and rivulets that curl and meander round the mountains. The air was filled with the noise of branches creaking, feet shuffling, leaves rustling, insects humming, wolves baying, wild boar snarling, jackles howling and leopards growling. The combined scent of vegetation, moisture, soil and decaying plants and wood assaulted their nostrils with the fear of death.

The Shivbharat Ch 20/33-38 says that *"the elephants particularly suffered. The ups and downs were so steep that the skin of the joints were bruised and battered. While climbing up they would hold on to the trees with their trunks. Inspite of that they slipped and fell into the ravines crushing many troops in the process.*

The standards and parasols were torn to shreds while passing through the bamboo islands. The riders got off the horses to decrease the load but still the horses found it difficult to climb."

Shivaji Raje is said to have made a road. Under this pretext Shivaji Raje had placed his men (mawlas) all along the road. These mawlas made a road by cutting trees but at the same time closed all the other tracks and routes. Because of this, unknown to Afzal khan there was only one way in and the same way out of Jawli.

Mawlas are the inhabitants of Mawal (Fig 1/4) They are the sons of the soil of the Sahyadris. They are a lean and wiry race. Not very tall but extremely tough and battle hardened. Living in the hills they are born rock climbers and excelled in mountain warfare. Their diet was very frugal, dried coconut, jaggery, puffed rice (pohe) and ground nut.

Afzal Khan reaches Jawli

On 07 November 1659, an exhausted Afzal Khan reached Jawli with his army of 15,000, and camped at Peth-Par for three days ie 7, 8, 9 November. This area was an ideal camping ground for 15,000 troops. The nearby Koyna river assured an ample supply of water to quench the thirst of both man and beast. The forest provided enough scrub and brushwood for the horses and elephants. The fatigued troops gave a sigh of relief after the laborious and precarious trek of Radtondi ghat.

All along the road and especially at the camping sites, Shivaji Raje was an excellent host. The physically drained army was pampered as though they were royal guests. The cuisine must have been mouth watering, and included fish, flesh and fowl. The Adilshahi army glutted and gorged on exotic sweet meats. It is possible that this made Afzal Khan's army lethargic and complacent. The news that a treaty is to take place must have made them cocksure and careless.

However Shivaji Raje had cunningly made alcoves and recesses for his sentinels to come close to Afzal Khan's camps and made hiding places in nooks and corners at every bend in the path. Shivaji Raje had his men around the camps in the guise of laborers helping the troops of Afzal Khan. These spies picked up tidbits of information and conveyed them to Shivaji Raje.

Morale of the Maratha camp 1-9 November

The morale of Shivaji Raje 's troops was not high.

His advisers doubted the sincerity of Afzal Khan keeping in mind his past history of cruelty and treachery.

They also knew that Afzal Khan was a massively built strong man. He could easily overpower two or three men single-handedly. Comparatively Shivaji Raje was slim and slightly built. The Chitnis Bakhar says- *Khan was as broad as a door, while Shivaji Maharaj was like the waxing crescent of the moon.*

There was also a selfish angle, they were scared: *if Shivaji Raje was imprisoned or killed, then what would happen to their services and watans?*

CHAPTER FIVE

Shivaji Raje's strategy prior to the meet- November 7,8,9.

Most of Shivaji Raje's advisers were in favour of a treaty. His ministers and sardars advocated a policy of appeasement. This was the largest army that had they had faced.

However Shivaji Raje knew the history of Afzal Khan's behaviour with the Bhosle family. He had brought his father Shahaji Raje in chains from Jinji to Bijapur. He had also caused the death of Shivaji Raje's elder brother Sambhaji at Kanakgiri.

The death of Shivaji Raje's elder brother Sambhaji.

According to the E.K. Chronicle Sambhaji eldest son of Shahaji Raje was struck by a cannon ball during a campaign against the Chief of Kanakgiri. This was due to some treachery by Afzal Khan. We also know from Muhammad Adilshah's Farman dated 20th March 1655 that the campaign against the Nayak of Kanakgiri was concluded by that date.

The Sabhasad Chronicle says when Shivaji Raje set out to meet Afzal Khan, Jijabai urged him to avenge the death of Sambhaji elder brother of Shivaji Raje.

When Shivaji Raje's counsellors advised him to make peace with Afzal Khan, Shivaji Raje told them that Afzal might kill him the way he killed Sambhaji, and that he would rather be killed in the attempt to eliminate the Khan than ever make peace with him.

Shivaji Raje's son, also named Sambhaji, was born 14th May 1657. No wonder, the death of Shahji's son, Sambhaji played an important role in the decision of Shivaji Raje to confront Afzal Khan.

This was the most critical moment in the life and career of Shivaji Raje.

If he capitulated to Afzal Khan, all his hopes of independence and future glory would be gone for ever, and he would have to end his days as a tame vassal of Bijapur.

If he confronted Afzal Khan now, he would have to take on the power of the Adilshahi, the Qutubshahi and the Mughals.

Shivaji Raje himself was in a terrible dilemma. He pondered on his life's choice and then chose the manlier though dangerous path. He decided to take Afzal Khan head on.

The Shivbharat Ch 20 / 10-13 tells us that the care-worn chieftain's sleep was broken by a vision of the goddess Bhavani who urged him to confront Afzal boldly and promised him victory and her full protection. This must have helped him make his bold decision. It definitely raised the morale of the Marathas.

Shivaji Raje had an oracle of Goddess Bhawani. The oracle was that *"Thirty two toothed goat (i.e. man / Afzal Khan) has walked in for sacrifice"* and Bhawani Devi had handed him a sword. The goddess Bhavani urged him to confront Afzal boldly promised him victory and her full protection. This was a good omen which spread widely among the troops,

The Shivbharat says in Ch 20/ 12-20:

The Devi said "a Muslim demon by the name of Afzal Khan has come to fight you. He is as cunning as Ravan .Kill him . I have come from Tulzapur to help you. Consider him dead. The Devbhumi should see his body drenched in blood, his head severed from his body, his arms separated from his body, his legs spread out, the jackals, dogs, vultures and crows pulling out his entrails. So saying the Bhavani Devi entered his sword."

There is a reference to Goddess Bhavani many times later also in his life. Even when Jaisingh came in 1665 the Goddess advised him to make a treaty with him. She assured him that though he would loose a large number of his forts, it would be a temporary loss of forts and face. He would soon get back both his forts and his pride. In fact he would emerge stronger after this ordeal.

During this period Shivaji Maharaj had called a meeting to discuss the preparation of the interview with Afzal Khan. It was attended by Gomaji Naik -Pansambal, Krishnaji Naik, Sumanji Naik, Nilopant, Annajipant, Sonopant, Gangaji Mangaji, Mankoji Dahatonde and Krishnaji Gaikwad.

At this brain storming Krishnaji Gaikwad advised Shivaji Raje to wear a armor under his tunic and a helmet under his turban. He was also advised to conceal a set of steel claws (waghnakh) fastened to his fingers by a pair of rings. In his right sleeve he hid a thin sharp dagger called a *bichuwa* (scorpion ie a double curved and double edged six inch dagger)

During the meeting it was suggested that Afzal Khan would grapple with Shivaji Raje and so Shivaji Raje practiced wrestling with a mawla about the size of Afzal Khan. There was so much attention to detail that one of the advisers thought that Shivaji Maharaj had too long a beard and Afzal Khan may take a grip on it. So it was trimmed.

This preparation for a hand to hand duel was the Seventh Turning point.

The morale of the troops of Afzal Khan on 7,8,9 November

Afzal Khan left his artillery behind at Wai.

The mountainous terrain of Jawli had immobilized the cavalry.

The talks were going on between the envoys Afzal Khan and Shivaji Raje and a meeting was arranged. A meeting meant a treaty ie there would be no war and therefore no bloodshed. But Afzal Khan was confident of his success.

As per the Shivabharat Ch 20/ 44-47,

"When the mighty Afzal Khan came near Jawli he felt as if he had already conquered it. When Shivaji Raje learnt that the Khan was near Jawli, he knew that he was now in his clutches."

The Adilshahi army encamped near a village by the name of Par, on the banks of the Koyna River. Both Shivaji Raje and Afzal Khan sent their respective envoys to inquire after one another's well being.

The Shivabharat Ch 20 / adds,

"Shivaji Raje perceived what was passing through the Khan's mind, the Khan guessed what Shivaji Maharaj was contemplating; but only the Almighty knew what was really happening. The common people assumed a treaty was in the offing."

A The 'Time frame' has been depicted in Fig 5/ 1.

Krishnaji Bhaskar had gone to Pratapgad once. He started for the visit on 9 October and returned on 17 October. Pantaji Gopinath was with him. He made two more trips and finally accompanied Afzal Khan and his troops to Peth-Par on 6th-7th Nov. The meeting was planned on 10th November. Between 5th and 8th Nov, besides Krishnaji Bhaskar and Pantaji Gopinath the ten bodyguards from each side must have checked the site and the approaches from an ambush point of view. Bada Sayed and Jiva Mahala both must have concentrated on the possibilities of treachery inside the shamiana.

Shivaji Raje did not have a mobile artillery nor light guns (Sutarnala ie rockets), nor men with personal guns (Bandookchi). His troops did not have any armor. Swords and spears were their main arms. But Shivaji Raje made amends by getting Afzal Khan's troops in an inconvenient place and making them complacent. Shivaji Raje's troops were well disciplined and battle hardened.

Earlier the troops had been tested in the battle of Purandar for quick manoeuvres. This time Shivaji Raje brought 15,000 troops of Trambak Bhaskar, Moro Pant and Shamraj Padmanabhi in a very short time and without rousing any suspicion and concentrated them against the main troops of Afzal Khan in the Koyana valley. This compensated for all the short comings in other departments.

Pantaji must have gone to Pratapgad to brief Shivaji Raje of the latest inputs and returned to Par on 9th Nov. It will be seen that Afzal Khan's men like Bada Sayyed had gone round the area but did not find anything suspicious. This speaks very high of the discipline of Shivaji Maharaj's troops. Shivaji Raje must have finalized his plan after the last trip of Pantaji.

Readying for the encounter.

No one could predict as to how the meeting would end. Except Afzal Khan who was convinced of his victory. To him it was very simple.

As per the protocol of the meeting, he was sure to have a few minutes alone with Shivaji Raje and in this time he could he would squeeze the neck and smother the life out of Shivaji Raje. Even if Shivaji Raje created a hue and cry he was sure that Bada Sayed could handle Jiva Mahala.

Time frame of the visits of Shivaji Raje, Pantaji, Krishnaji and Afzal Khan

Even if the Jiva Mala - Bada Sayed fracas lasted longer his ten bodyguards would keep Shivaji Raje's ten bodyguards occupied for enough time for him to complete his job ie to strangulate the upstart Shiva.

It goes to the credit of Shivaji Raje that he was very pragmatic and he thought of the following possibilities.

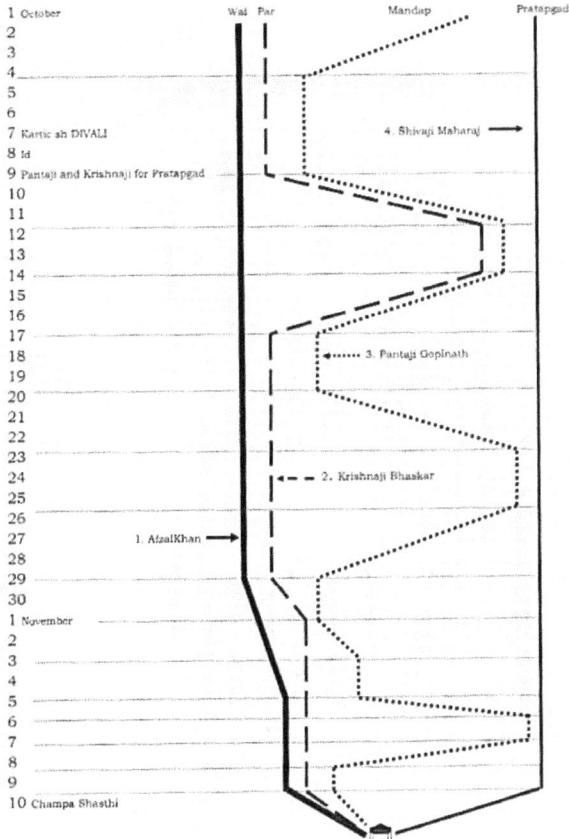

Fig 5/1

Eight possible options at the meeting.

1. Death of Shivaji Raje.

2. Death of Afzal Khan.

3. Afzal Khan injured.

4. Afzal Khan becoming a prisoner.

5. Shivaji Raje getting injured.

6. Shivaji Raje becoming a prisoner.

7. Treaty concurred.

8. Afzal Khan or /and Shivaji Raje dead /alive but Bijapur army takes Pratapgad.

In the case of option -1 ie Death of Shivaji Raje.

In case of his death, Shivaji Raje said "...*Swarajya to be continued by declaring Sambhaji as the King and Jijabai as the regent. Kanhoji Jedhe would be in charge of the army ....*"

In case of option – 2, Afzal Khan's death and Shivaji Raje 's victory, it is well known that, a signal was decided ie firing of cannon, so that all the troops would attack Afzal Khan's army.

In the case of option -3/4, Afzal Khan being injured or being a prisoner the same signal was to be given.

The Jedhe Chronology records Shivaji Raje's instructions to the Bandal and Shilimbkar contingents:

"In a confidential meeting that Shivaji Raje held with his ministers and Kanhoji Jedhe, it was agreed that the Muslim (Afzal Khan) is perfidious. The Bandal Deshmukh with his force will be in Jawli and in the forest of Par. If the Khan should act treacherously during the meeting, the Bandal Deshmukh should not let the Khan's army camped in Par ascend the mountain (fort), and support me (Shivaji Raje) with select men. If, by the blessings of goddess Shri Amba, Afzal Khan is killed, the Bandals will attack and thoroughly destroy the enemy army in Par after receiving a signal from the fort. Haibatrao and Balaji Naik Shilimbkar are positioned in the Bochegholi pass with their troops. They will not let the enemy ascend the pass. Thus it was resolved and arranged in the secret meeting."

The instructions in case of 6/ 7 were very clear to Kanhoji Jedhe "......*and if I become a prisoner, you and your group should fight and I should be taken in your mob. After I join you, we will destroy the enemy....*".

It is therefore surmised that Shivaji Raje must have given instructions in case of all the possibilities given above.

Kanhoji had the most difficult part to play as he had to take decisions as per the outcome of the interview between Shivaji Raje and Afzal Khan's.

In case of option -2, if Shivaji Raje killed Afzal Khan -The cannons would be fired at Pratapgad fort. This would be the signal for the complete army to attack. Netoji in particular was supposed to strike at the Adilshahi base at Wai.

In case of option -5, if Shivaji Raje was wounded, Kanhoji would determine the plan of action.

In case of option -6, if Shivaji Raje was imprisoned.

If Shivaji Raje was imprisoned and this was a possibility both sides had thought of. The Adilshahi army had a wooden cage ready, in case Shivaji Raje was brought as a prisoner. They had planned to take him like a wild animal. First, he would be handed over to the 1200 Habashi troops stationed between the Par and the shamiana. Shivaji Raje would have been brought by Afzal Khan and his bodyguards from the Mandap to the location of the Habashi troops. It was at that moment Kanhoji would ambush the party which was taking the imprisoned Shivaji Raje.

All the troops of Bandals, Shilimbkars, Annaji Rangnath should start attack on all sides to divert the attention of the Habashi troops, and thus save the small but the utmost important group of Kanhoji whose duty was to protect Shivaji Raje from an accumulative attack by the Habashi troops.

In case of option – 7, if there was a treaty.

If there was a treaty between Afzal Khan and Shivaji Raje, withdrawal of the troops was required, that too without any clashes. The most critical situation would have arisen, if there was to be a treaty or understanding between Afzal Khan and Shivaji Raje. To take back 30,000 troops by Shivaji Raje would have been a very delicate task. To deploy them would have taken one and a half day. To go back would need three days. Should this be noticed by the Dabhol troops or by Siddi of Janjira, they would have definitely advanced. Again Netoji was away at Raireshwar and Jor valley, and if not informed properly would attack Wai. The troops of Afzal Khan in the Koyana valley could have got a hint and attacked. Their artillery would decimate the Maratha troops. Therefore, Shivaji Raje must have decided about a signal for withdrawal also.

But both sides knew that the possibility of a treaty was very, very minimal.

In case of option -8, Afzal Khan could die but the Bijapur army could take Pratapgad Fort.

We must realise that Afzal Khan had not come to Jawli with the intention to formulate a treaty .His intention was to kill the upstart Shivaji Raje and then to capture the whole of Shivaji Raje's territory .He was supremely confident that he could strangulate Shivaji Raje with his bare hands and after he did that, his ten bodyguards would fend off Shivaji Raje's ten body guards .The 1200 Habshis whom he had brought and stationed at Par would rush from there and attack the Pratapgad fort . His information on the 09 November was that the fort had a garrison of not more than 2000 soldiers. True they were at a higher ground but he had shutarmals mounted on camels. He had left most of his elephants at Wai but he had brought some of them to Par. They had arrived bruised and injured but they still could be useful to barge open the fort's doors.

The distance between Pratapgad and Par was 500 metres. Today ie in 2024 the record for a 500 metre Olympic dash is about 50 seconds ie about one minute.

The Habshis were battle hardened elite troops of Afzal Khan and they must have been supremely fit. But each of them was weighed down by by a sword, a dagger, a shield and a spear each. Also they were running uphill. Assuming that they were thirty times slower, the main body would be at the Shamiana in maximum 15 minutes.

The soldiers with artillery would take some more time to organize themselves ie about half an hour to one hour. As we have already discussed two men could easily carry one shutarmal and a camel could carry two shutarmals.

Thus besides all the possibilities and alternatives described above, Kanhoji had the task of not allowing Afzal Khan's Habshi troops at Par to climb the hill and attack the fort. Because even if Afzal Khan was killed and yet the Habshis took Pratapgad, it would be a certain victory for the Adilshahi.

10 November 1659 : 6.00 AM to 1.00 PM

San Tzu (544 - 496 BC) was a Chinese general, strategist and philosopher who wrote the Art of War. He said that, for a general to be successful in the drama of war, his first duty is to study carefully the theatre of operations so that he may see clearly the relative advantages and disadvantages it presents for himself and his enemies.

Sadly Afzal Khan had banked on his brute might rather than the subtleties of war.

Many historians have emphasized on the use of terrain as force multipliers which Shivaji Raje did.

Shivaji Raje had 30,000 troops encircling Afzal khan's 15,000 troops. The Maratha troops were close enough to ambush but far enough to be concealed, ie about 200 metres distance. These troops had assembled in the morning and concealed themselves at their appointed nooks, corners, on tree tops, small caves and crevices by the time meeting was to take place. After all it was the land of their forefathers, land they had grown up in and they knew it like the back of their hand. Every man was straining to fall upon the invaders and annihilate the enemy, on the signal of the five cannon shots. It was not a passive waiting or patience. It was active concentration of strength waiting to strike and take revenge for the atrocities committed by the Adilshahi on the Marathas.

The position of the shamiana was on the ridge going from the fort towards Kumbharoshi village, about 500 metres from the now named Abdulla Buruj.

Afzalkhan got up in the morning and must have given last minute instructions to his army. They were most likely to be orders about how to celebrate the killing of Shivaji Raje. Perhaps he must have commanded his officers to check whether the cage was in order.

Afzal Khan :1.00 PM to 1.30 PM.

Afzal Khan must have dressed up in all his finery, carried a Katyar (dagger) and a sword and then, got into his palanquin and started overconfidently for the shamiana.

Shivaji Raje also got ready, he wore his armor and a helmet and a dress over it, inserted Waghnakh (tiger claws) in the fingers of left palm, a bhichwa (short curved knife) in his left sleeve and tied a sword to his waist.

Ten body guards of each, would be standing some fifteen metres away ready to strike at the slightest provocation. They all could see what is happening in the shamiana. Shivaji Raje's troops on Pratapgad could see what was happening around the shamiana.

The time of the meet was around the third part of the day i.e. two hours past mid-day. (2.00 PM).

Afzal Khan would have come up along a track from Peth-Par. With him, would be two envoys Krishnaji Bhaskar and Pantaji Gopinath, 10 body guards and 1,200 Habashi troops. The moment they reached the place where the troops were to halt, Pantaji pointed out this fact to Afzal Khan and Afzal Khan ordered his troops to halt. This place can be identified as a small plain on the ridge, about 400 metres away from the shamiana. Afzal Khan then started further and in about one to one and half Ghatika (some thirty minutes) arrived at the shamiana. (See Map 4/6) in about 15 minutes. He then climbed up the platform and entered the luxurious shamiana. Once seated he looked around and was shocked at its opulence.

The shamiana was an intriguing affair. Annaji Ranganath Malkare built this shamiana.

Though how and from where Shivaji Raje got this luxurious shamiana throws up a lot of questions. Because Shivaji Raje led a frugal life and he was not bogged down by dancing women, cannons or elephants or large tents.

The shamiana was built on a platform about 10 by 10 metres. The height of the platform was about 50 centimetres so that one had to exert himself to climb it.

The shamiana was decorated with gorgeous carpets and cushions worthy of a royal guest. The cushions must have been made of silk and mulmul, with lace and frills. The pillows must have been embroidered and incorporated with pearls and beads.

Looking at this pomp and grandeur, Afzal Khan was astonished and said *"even the Patshah did not did not have such a luxurious shamiana"* hearing this Pantaji had replied *"All things of Patshah will go to Patshah only"*. In fact he also remarked that it was the first sign of Shivaji Raje's submission and the pains that Shivaji Raje had taken, showed how highly Shivaji Raje respected Afzal Khan.

Shivaji Raje: 1.00 PM to 1.30 PM.

Shivaji Raje also started from Pratapgad to meet his destiny.

The Shivabharat Ch 21/11-18 describes the scene thus:

"Shivaji Raje began preparing for the meeting after learning that Afzal Khan had started towards the meeting place at the foot of the Pratapgad Fort. He worshipped Lord Shiva in various ways as advised by the priests, gave away alms as per daily routine, had a light lunch, sipped pure water from time to

time, silently prayed for a moment to goddess Tulaja, dressed appropriately for the occasion and glanced at the reflection of his face in a mirror. He made obeisance to the priest and other Brahmins and obtained their blessing. He viewed the Sun and then gave away a cow along with her calf and some gold in alms to a virtuous Brahmin. He secretly positioned his brave followers, who were eager to go with him, for the defence of Pratapgad fort. Then he left to receive the Muslim (Afzal Khan) who had come there with treachery in mind, as amicably as somebody welcomes his guest. Shivaji Raje had donned excellent armor (under his robe). He was wearing a white turban with a hackle and a robe sprinkled with saffron. With a sword in one hand and a patta (long sword) in the other, he looked like Lord Vishnu incarnate who bears a sword in one hand and a mace in the other. Shivaji Raje, pacing briskly, descended the fort on foot."

The moment Shivaji Raje started from the fort. It was a signal for his troops to start moving to the battle positions. Silently and stealthily the troops moved to their final positions.

At about 1.45 PM, the Maratha troops were poised to strike in next 15 minutes.

Afzal Khan's troops awaited the declaration of a treaty or Shivaji Raje to be brought in chains or his corpse. They were unaware of the closing in movement of Shivaji Raje's troops.

The meeting was in the third part of the day. As per protocol number seven, Afzal Khan was the elder of the two and therefore it was deemed that Shivaji Raje would come and pay his respects. The waiting from March to November had frustrated him and all he wanted was to do was kill Shiva (ji) and get done with it. He was so impatient he arrived much earlier than the designated time. The palki was brought by bhois (laborers carrying the palki) and parked it nearby. Afzal Khan got down and climbed the houda (platform) in the shamiana and made himself comfortable.

As per protocol number four the 10 bodyguards from both sides also took their position at range of an arrow shot. Both the envoys stood in the mandap.

Shivaji Raje started from fort Pratapgad and walked the long slow walk. He had 100 metres extra distance to walk. He was deliberately walking slowly to show that he was very scared. After all even courageous persons were scared of Afzal Khan.

Shivaji Raje walked upto the place where his 10 bodyguards were to take up positions and stopped in his tracks. He was shocked to see Bada Sayyad moving around in the shamiana. This was clearly a breach of protocol number three ie *"in the shamiana, besides the envoys there would be no other person."*

Bada Sayyed was a master of the Dandpatta. Shivaji Raje required a person who was equally pro efficient in wielding the Dandpatta. He found one in Jiva Mahala. Shivaji Raje's instructions to Jiva were very clear. He was supposed to concentrate and kill Bada Sayed . Regardless of what occurred around him ie to Shivaji Raje, he was supposed to concentrate only and only on Bada Sayyed.

Shivaji Raje sent a *harkari* (messenger) and called for Pantaji and brought this to his notice who in turn pointed out this breach in protocol to Afzal Khan. Whether this was a mistake or a deliberate act, one does not know for certain. But it must be remembered that Pantaji had to insist that the 1200 Habshi could not accompany Afzal Khan to the shamiana .

An exasperated Afzal Khan then ordered Bada Sayyad to go and stand at his assigned place, away from the shamiana.

With Bada Sayyad shifted out of the immediate arena, Shivaji Raje walked towards the platform. It was precisely at this time that Yesaji Kank with his 40 men must have stealthily surrounded the shamiana.

When Shivaji Raje continued the long slow walk to the shamiama, he knew he was entering a lion's den. And while he did so the eyes of every Maratha in Jawli was on him.

The Shivaji Raje -Afzal Khan Meeting : 2.00 PM to 2.15 PM

When Shivaji Raje stood near the platform, the formal introductions took place. Krishnaji pointed to him and said to Afzal Khan *"This is Shivaji Raje"*.

Pantaji then pointed out to Shivaji Raje that, *"This is Afzal Khan"*.

Shivaji Raje was well aware of the hugeness of Afzal Khan but Afzal Khan was aghast on seeing this pigmy like thin and slim creature called Shiva(ji) j. He was amazed that he come with an army of 60,000 for this tini mini upstart Maratha.

After this greeting Shivaji Raje with the right show of fear climbed the houda. As he entered Afzal Khan rose expectantly from his seat and advanced towards him, as would a stalker towards his prey .

In order to make Shivaji Raje complacent the Khan handed over his sword to Krishnaji and in the tone of a elder admonishing a naughty young boy, he said *"Oh! You who pretend to be eager for war and act in an extremely willful manner! You have treaded the wrong path and, in your vanity, demonstrate no respect for the Adilshah, the Qutbshah or the mighty Mughal Emperor. I have come to chastise you for your arrogance. Give up these mountain forts and your greed and surrender to me. I will personally conduct you to Bijapur, make you bow before the victorious master, Ali Adilshah, make an entreaty to him on your behalf and have him bestow great wealth on you. Oh! Son of Shahaji! Child! Rid yourself of pride in your wisdom and let me take your hand in mine. Come, embrace me."*

Shivaji Raje was aware that Afzal Khan did not put away his sword to calm him. He did this because a sword which is 2 to 2.5 feet long, was of no use in close combat .

In a hand to hand fight it was the dagger that was more important and lethal.

He must have come to know this after his several bouts with a Maratha mawla of the size of Afzal Khan.

But he also decided to play along and he too handed over his sword to his envoy Pantaji.

The Embrace : 2.15 PM to 3.00 PM

Fig 5/2

So saying Afzal Khan spread out his hands. The span seemed to engulf the entire shamiana . Shivaji Raje's head only came up to Afzal Khan's shoulders.

Then they both embraced. First they both swayed to their respective left made body contact and then they drew apart. Afzal Khan being a tall man his arms reached Shivaji Raje's neck while Shivaji Raje's arms and forearm came round his torso lower down.

Next they swayed to their respective right and suddenly Afzal Khan rotated his torso first clockwise and then anti clockwise. With a quick turning movement he clasped Shivaji Raje's neck in his left armpit in an iron grip and squeezed it.

After that he drew his dagger with his right hand plunged it into Shivaji Raje's abdomen from the left side. But it did not sink in as Shivaji Raje had worn his armor under his garment. The dagger only scraped the mailed armor. This must given Afzal Khan his first shock.

Before the surprised Afzal Khan could react Shivaji Raje who was almost strangulated by Afzal Khan's left armpit, then stabbed Afzal Khan's abdomen with his *waghnakh*. Then he dragged the tiger claws across the abdomen which had sunk in about a centimeter deep.

This was the second shock that Afzal Khan got. The pain was enough to make him wince and slacken his grip on Raje's neck. The over confident Afzal Khan had not worn any armor. Afzal Khan must have realized that something had gone horribly wrong. He tried to push away Shivaji Raje, but inspite of Afzal Khan's strength Shivaji Raje held on to him.

Relieved from the strangulation, Shivaji Raje then with his right hand took out a bichwa (scorpion like dagger with double curved six inch blade) from his left sleeve and rammed the shaft of the bichwa into Afzalkhan's soft opulent abdomen. After Shivaji Raje had plunged the bichwa upto the hilt, he did not just make a vertical stab wound but made a slicing horizontal hara-kiri like movement with so much power that he slit open Afzal Khan's abdomen. The slit was broad enough for Shivaji Raje to insert his fingers into Afzal Khan's abdomen and pull Afzal Khan's intestines out.

During this time a furious and astonished Afzal Khan must have roared in pain and agony, thrown away the katiyar in his right fist. He must have brought his palms down to the level of Shivaji Raje's chest and tried to push him away. Or may be Shivaji Raje must have backed away on his own, perhaps surprised at how well he has executed his own plan. A mortally wounded Afzal Khan, clutching his intestines, stumbled out of the shamiana and made a desperate attempt to go towards his palkhi. Trying to push back his *kothala* (bowels) into the lacerated wound he shouted *"Daga Daga". Treachery, treachery. This enemy has killed me. Kill this enemy immediately)*

Sabhasad agrees with the above:

" the Khan pressed Shivaji Raje's neck under his left arm and struck a blow with his dagger in Shivaji Raje's side. The agile Shivaji Raje worked himself free of the Khan's grasp, parried the stroke of the dagger and drove his own sword into the Khan's stomach. The Khan, stunned by the blow, tried to hold his entrails with his hands and cried out that he had been killed. His servant suddenly rushed at Shivaji Raje with the Khan's sword poised for a stroke. The Khan had included this man in his entourage knowing well that Shivaji Raje would never kill a Brahmin. Shivaji Raje parried the stroke with his sword and, using his patta, cleft the Khan's head into two....."

Thus on Thursday noon, 10th November 1659, Shivaji Raje slew the enemy of the gods, Afzal Khan."

Meanwhile Bada Sayyad realized that his master Afzal Khan was mortally wounded. He sprang into action and charged towards Shivaji Raje, but Jiva Mahala who was tasked to watch him and *him alone* easily tackled him and chopped off his hand with his dandpatta (long sword) and then killed him.

Similarly each and every one of Khan's other nine other body guards who had been *'mapped and marked Man to Man'* at the shamiana were systematically killed.

Shivbharat Ch 21/53-55 describes the macabre scene.

'The head of Afzal Khan lay fallen on one side while his body lay else where, the intestines were scattered somewhere else while his (head gear) patka lay elsewhere, his parasol was lay on one side while his fly whisker lay else where and his shirpech (turban crest) had fallen aside.

Thus due to his beastly actions, his body, his clothes and his ornaments lay scattered hither and thither.'

Was there a treachery? Who used the weapon first?

'There was no treachery. Both warriors were allowed to carry arms.'

It is thought that if Afzal Khan had worn an armor, he could not have been stabbed. But logic says that it would have been possible to do so inspite of an armor. Since Shivaji Raje was short as compared to Afzal Khan his hands easily encircled Afzal Khan's abdomen. Shivaji Raje could easily slip the palm of his hand carrying *waghnakh or bichwa* under the armor and pull out the intestines.

Who used weapon first? All the Marathi documents are unanimous that Afzal Khan used his weapon first but failed as Shivaji Raje had worn his armor.

As Sir Jadunath puts it very pithily- *'Diamond cuts diamond.'*

Trumpets at 3.00 PM.

By this time Shivaji Raje's trumpeters (shingya) blew the trumpets in a particular pre determined way. This was a signal to the Maratha garrison in the fort and the army nearby that,

1. That the meeting had taken place.

2 Shivaji Raje had slain Afzal Khan

3. They were supposed to burst out of their hiding places and pounce on the Bijapuri army.

Now the nine bodyguards of both the sides assaulted each other. Yesaji Kank with his 40 men also joined the clash. Grossly out numbered Afzal Khan's nine bodyguards were killed by these 50 mawlas.

The bhois placed the mortally wounded Afzal Khan and tried to take him away to safety. The Adnyandas powada says in verse 33 - Sambhaji Kavji noticed this and immediately first chopped of the legs of the bhois and then severed the head of Afzal Khan. Clutching it by his hair he joined Shivaji Raje and his bodyguards and ran back to the fort. The moment Shivaji Raje and his men entered the fort, the gates of the fort were closed. As decided Shivaji Raje ordered the cannons to be fired. All this action would have taken about one hour ie Shivaji Raje returned back to Pratapgad at about 3.00 pm.

(Note :The sound of a trumpet is about 100 decibels and like the sound of a car horn

It can be heard about 500 metres away.

The sound of a medieval cannon stone shot was about 175-200 decibels and the blast could be heard about 15 km away.)

Krishna Bhaskar.

After Afzal Khan the man who was most startled by Shivaji Raje's actions was Krishnaji Bhaskar, as he was in the shamiana itself.

One version says that he had the sword given to him by Afzal Khan and he instinctively aimed a blow at Shivaji Raje but missed. Since Krishnaji was a Brahmin, Shivaji Raje spared him and allowed him to go away.

However, another version says that Shivaji Raje did not kill him because he was a Brahmin; but he was killed by Jiva Mahala.

There is still another version that Krishnaji Bhaskar aimed a blow with his sword on Shivaji Raje's forehead. But Shivaji Raje was wearing a jiretop (helmet) and it made a very small wound. In fact it is said that both Fazal Khan at Panhalgad and Jijamata after the escape from Agra identified Shivaji Raje on the basis of the scar of this wound.

However there is no mention of Krishnaji Bhaskar later in the Shivabharat which indicates that he was most probably killed. Sabhasad writes:

"The Raja (Shivaji Raje) himself killed in single combat the Khan who was by nature a veritable Duryodhan; as much in strength of body as in wickedness of heart. Bhima killed him single-handed. Similarly did [the Raja]. Shivaji Raje was Bhima himself. It was he who killed Afzal. This deed was not that of a

human being. An incarnation he surely was, and so indeed could he perform this deed. Success was attained."

Adnyandas in his powada (ballad), expressing a similar sentiment, says that Shivaji Raje was an incarnation of God, like Rama who single handedly killed Ravana.

The road from Par to the foot of Pratapgad was an uphill slope. Shivaji Raje's troops on Pratapgad could clearly see what was happening near the shamiana and accordingly take action. But Afzal Khan's troops 500 metres below, could not see the action that took place as the sun was in their eyes. So they and consequently the rest of Afzal Khan s army remained blissfully ignorant of the blood bath that took place at the shamiana ..

About 60 minutes after the Afzal Khan and Shivaji Raje confrontation, trumpets were sounded. When the trumpets had sounded, the Adilshahi troops felt that they heralded the triumphant victory of Afzal Khan. The Habshi troops awaited the jubilant arrival of Afza Khan with Shivaji Raje in tow either as a corpse or as prisoner. They stood there to present a Guard of Honour. The wooden cage, that Pantaji had seen was kept ready, in case Afzal Khan had managed to capture Shivaji Raje alive.

Cannons fired at 3.15 PM.

At about 3.00 pm the Habshis heard the gun salvo and they perhaps thought that Pratapgad fort was taken. But the Maratha troops knew that Shivaji Raje had killed Afzal Khan and reached the fort in safety. This was a clarion call for an all out attack. The Adilshahi army were flabbergasted that the so called frightened Maratha army was suddenly pouncing on them from all sides.

We have already seen that Shivaji Raje had analysed and discussed the tactics to be deployed in all the eight possibilities. We have also seen that Kanhoji Jedhe was deputed by Shivaji Raje to decide the action to be taken as per the situation.

After an hour (from 2:00 to 3:00 PM) of intense suspense the cannons sounded. All the pent up pressure built up over the past six-seven months was suddenly released. Kanhoji drew his sword, gave the Maratha War-cry: "Har Har Mahadev", and his 100 men attacked the Habashi troops.

The Habashi troops must have been astonished at the audacity of a Maratha sardar with only a hundred men to attack such well armed 1200 Habashi troops? They must have had a second surprise when the very next moment 4,000 to 5,000 Maratha troops were seen coming from all the sides like a swarm of ants. The Habashis must have had no time to load their muskets or even to draw their swords. The Marathas attacking them were troops of Shilimbkar, Bandal and Annaji Ranganath. All these troops had hidden from the previous day in Bocheghali and other nallas. It must have been a bloody hand-to-hand fighting. The Habashi troops were in a tight battle order formation. All Habashis must have been killed or wounded.

Afzal Khan's main army at Par must have heard the noise and must have felt that the troops are rejoicing. Before they could realise anything, the Maratha troops led by Moropant must have pounced on them.

The Adilshahi army could not use their Artillery or Cavalry. The Marathas had moved too close. There was no time to load the guns, nor time to mount saddles. The Marathas spears were coming at them thick and fast. The Bandukchis had no time to load their weapons. The Adilshahi army was in utter chaos.

CHAPTER SIX

The Battle of Koyana.

One day before the meet, Shivaji Raje's troops in Pratapgad area were as follows, Pratapgad 2,000; at Par- Bandal and Shilimbkar 2,000; Kanhoji Jedhe around Pratapgad 3,000 and Dharkaris at Jawli 4,000 to 5,000. Each *buruj* (tower) of the *gad* (fort) was occupied and all Mets (posts) around were occupied. In the night before the meet, Bandal and Shilimbkar must have moved to Bocheghali and to the required place, Kanhoji also had stealthily moved his troops in the night to the hide outs around the Habashis' positions.

In the night, Moropant with 5,000 troops had come and occupied the positions at Par, Shamraj Padmanabhi with 5,000 troops came down to Koyana from Makarandgad area, Trambak Bhaskar with 5,000 troops reached Jawli from Mahad Chandragad side, Raghunath Ballal with 1,000 troops came up from Jor valley to Kshetra Mahabaleshwar, where Babaji Bhosale was present with his 2,000 troops. They had reached the places by forced marches and rested for the night. While the Adilshahi army slept it did not know that a noose of was descending around their neck.

On the day of the meet, in the morning while they heard the fun fare of Afzal Khan, the Marathas must have started to their battle positions, which would be ten to fifteen minutes distance from Afzal Khan's troops. By the time trumpets were sounded in the shamiana to herald the actual meeting, the Maratha troops must have reached the battle positions. But Afzal Khan and his Urmaos were totally ignorant of this manoeuvre. There were also a number of Maratha soldiers in the camp under the guise of water carriers, cooks, fire wood cutters and other sundry workers. Most of Afzal Khan troops at Par were blissfully unaware that they were being attacked within the camp and from outside the camp by an army of 4000. Afzal Khan must have had sentries posted around his camp, but they must have become complacent when he started in the morning for the meeting with Shivaji Raje. When the trumpets sounded outside the shamiana, Afzal Khan's troops began to celebrate while Shivaji Raje's troops moved from concealment positions to attack mode. The attack started in the fourth part of the day. Being in the lower part of the valley, there was light only for 2 hours.

Kanhoji Jedhe, Bandal Shilimbkar and Annaji Rangnath with 5,000 troops destroyed 1,200 Habashi troops. Here Marathas had a four to one superiority. The Adilshahi army at Par was attacked by Moropant with 5,000 troops, and Shamraj Padmanabhi with 5000 troops encircling from the south and east side. These divisions were commanded by Kamloji Salunkhe, Tanaji Malusare, Kondaji Varkhal, Ramaji Pangara and Suryaji Katkar. In Koyana, Shivaji Raje had at least two to one superiority. More over the route for return of Afzal Khan's army was cut off by Raghunath Ballal and Babaji Bhosale. Kanhoji and his Mawles were on the west side of this army, attacking as well as not allowing Afzal Khan's troops to climb up Pratapgad. At Kumbharoshi, Trambak Bhaskar and his 5,000 Dharkaris attacked. Here also Marathas had two to one superiority. These troops encircled from the north and east side. Besides this, Raghunath Ballal and Babaji Bhosale had put up a road-block on the two tracks leading to Wai. The encirclement was complete.

Muse Khan who was Afzal Khan's second in command tried to counter attack but the Adilshahi army was completely routed. The carnage in the Bijapuri army was terrible. Adnyadas said "all who begged quarters holding grass between their teeth (as a mark of humility) were spared, the rest were put to sword." Some troops ran away to Wai. Many troops took the south route along the Koyana river.

If the Adilshahi army had a foreboding during the ominous trek from Mahabaleshwar to Pratapgad the post battle war zone had become chilling.

With the wind slipping through leaves, cracking undergrowth with each step, creaking tree trunks, the flutter of wings unseen, snapping twigs, grass and weed sliding against the legs, breathing sounds, fox yipping, wolves howling snarls, padding feet along a trail, a grunt of pain at tripping on a root.

It seems that, Fazal Khan, Yakut Khan and Muse Khan could get out by this route only with the help of Prataprao More.

Netoji's Attack on Wai.

Netaji's cavalry was at the Jor valley and the Raireshwar plateau (Map 4/3) He did not hear the five cannon shots. It was evening by the time he got the message. Netoji reached at Wai in the early morning. But it was too late.

Harkaras (runners) with the Adilshahi army at Koyna must have carried the news of the death of Afzal Khan to Wai. The news must have reached Wai at about eight p.m. The base at Wai was immediately evacuated, all the material, treasury, families, weapons, horses were sent back post haste. By mid-night the evacuation was complete and by morning they were safe at Chandan-Vandan.

Destruction of Afzal Khan's Army.

On 11 November Afzal Khan's confused army at Koyana was completely routed. Many reached Bijapur by various routes. The troops had to leave behind all the heavy baggage, food, fodder, provisions, elephants, horses, camels, oxen, cannons carts etc.

The figures given of the material and other items left behind by Afzal Khan's army are as follows:

Elephants	65-95	Horses	4000-14,000
Camels	1,200	Oxen	1,800
Guns	70-90	Cloth/ baggage	3,000

Treasury - Rs.1,10,000 to Rs. 7,00,000

Precious stones - Rs.3,00,000.

The loss of the troops was as follows.

Afzal Khan: Dead - 3,000, Injured / Imprisoned - 2,000 to 3,000

Shivaji Raje: Dead - 1,734, Injured 427

After the Battle.

After the battle, Shivaji Raje visited the battlefield next morning.

A list was made of all the dead and injured. All the prisoners were assembled, important prisoners like Zunzarrao Ghatge, Mambaji Bhosale, two sons of Afzal Khan, brothers of Rustum Jemah, Khandoji Khopade and Jagtap were released after taking due ranson.

1. All the loot was collected centrally and was accounted for.

2. All the dead were cremated or buried according to their religion.

3. The vatans of the dead were given to their heirs. Widows who had no son, were given half the vatan. All the persons who had shown exceptional bravery were given bracelets. The injured persons were given 50 to 100 Hons according to the nature of their wound. Also chains of pearls, trickles, necklaces, chains of gold, earrings, other ornaments, dresses, turbans and robes were distributed.

4. Children, ladies, brahmins, maulanas, non combatants and servants were released after giving them some money and rations.

We have already seen the important role that Kanhoji played in the first hour of the battle of Jawli. He had seven possibilities to consider and act accordingly. Even after Afzal Khan was killed the Habshi at Par could have attacked Pratapgad and taken it. It then would have led to an Adilshahi victory. In view of this exemplary courage Shivaji Raje conferred a battle honor *talwaricha mana cha argaman* (sword of honor) to the Jedhes.

There were many persons from the Adilshahi army who joined Shivaji Raje. Siddi Hilal, Pandhare and Kate changed over to Shivaji Raje.

Khandoji Khopade's one hand and one leg were cut, which we will discuss later.

Mannuchi

Mannuchi was a Venetian writer and a traveller who wrote an account of the Mughal Empire in his book Storia do Mogor. Mannuchi corroborates in principle all that has been described, though not very accurately as he was not actually present at the war zone. " .... *The king of Bijapur wrote to ShivaGi that his unruly conduct was not the way to respond to the benefits that had been conferred on his grandfather and were still being shown to his father and himself. He should desist from such courses and repair to the court, where an office could be given him; ShivaGi took no notice of this letter and continued his plundering more vigorously than before, so that the king of Bijapur, finding himself endangered because ShivaGi had taken one his fortresses, determined to send against him a famous general called Afzal Can. This man pursued ShivaGi so persistantly that the rebel was forced to take refuge in the mountains. Finding himself powerless for further resistance, he resorted to a trick, writing to Afzal Can a letter, in which he made excuses, confessed himself a criminal and culprit, and asked the general to intercede for him. He besought pardon from the king.*"

"Afzal Khan replied that he might come in without any hesitation, that he would obtain his Pardon from the King, and would be always under his protection. But he must appear without delay to obviate the receipt of fresh orders from the King, enjoining further exertions of defect and capture him. It would be better for himself and for the horrors of war. In any case, however he (ShiwaGi) could not desist long, the King being so much the more powerful."

" Shivaji consented to appear before Afzal Khan, but begged him to come with only five (actually ten)persons to a spot at a distance from the camp, while on his side he (Shivaji) would bring no more than five(ten) men. He would fall at his feet and throw himself up, Afzal Khan accepted his proposals. At a distance from the Camp he caused to be made ready a splendid tent with carpets for the reception of Shivaji, who on his side did not neglect to send message, imploring Afzal Khan's friendship and assurance of the petitioners being received with affection. "

"Meanwhile, he (Shivaji) so disposed his army for the carrying out of his plot that when he gave the agreed signal, all of them, spurring up their horses, would gallop straight into the royal camp. Shivaji got ready a small and very sharp lancet, which at the top was formed into the ring, the Lancet was concealed under cover of the hand. His five(ten) companions received orders that when he embraced the general the general, they would silently seize their swords and fall each upon one particular enemy. All the five (ten)men with their men with their leader, Shivaji, wore coats of mail beneath their clothes. This precaution was not adopted by Afzal Khan and his five(ten) men, nor did they suspect the treachery about to be practiced on them,"

"Afzal Khan was in his tent between the two armies, waiting with great anxiety for the arrival of Shivaji, and building fancy, many castles in the air. Then Shivaji appeared with his five men, all on horseback. At some distance from the tent they descended from their horses. Shivaji began to advance, bowing again and again, as if he was petitioning for a good reception and was in a state of apprehension. Afzal Khan beckoned to him with his hands that he might approach without fear; and as Shivaji drew near, Afzal Khan raised his arms as if to embrace him, Shivaji's hands came round his lower down, Afzal Khan being a tall man and very corpulent, then stabbed him with a small lancet, so that the bowels protruded. The other five men laid hold of their swords and cut *to pieces, Afzal Khan's companies. The appointment signal was given, and Shivaji's soldiers arriving, fell upon the army of Afzal Khan, and taken unawares it could not resist the impetus of Shivaji, more especially now its general was gone. Everything was thrown into confusion, and then men took to flight. But Shivaji had adopted measures by which the passes into the hills were already occupied by his soldiers, and thus the whole of the royal army was disposed of. He became more powerful than ever through the plunder at horses, arms and money that he acquired."*

(**Map 6/1**)

The whole incident is well and appropriately narrated in the Powada by Adnyandas,

> *'Like Hanuman and Angad to Lord Ram*
> *Jedhes and Bandals to Shivaji Raje.'*

Little suprise then that Shivaji Raje had conferred "Talvariche Pan" (order of sword) on the Jedhes.

The news of Afzal Khan's death and the total rout of the Adilshahi army reached Bijapur five days after the debacle at Pratapgad.

The most important feature of the Pratapgad campaign is the 'exploitation' after the victory. Shivaji Raje made good use of the chaos caused in Bijapur and made a three pronged attack.

Exploitation of the victory : 15 Forts in 17 days

Shivbharat Ch 23/ 58-61 says that, Shivaji Raje himself charged south wards and captured 15 forts ie Chandan, Vandan, Saswad, Supe, Shirval, Khatav, Waduz, Mayni, Kaledhon, Khanapur, Visapur, ,Tasgaon, Sangli, Ashti,Karad, Masur, Satara and thus became a master of a large territory of Bijapur, practically equal to his own area. In this, he captured the Sahyadri top extending about 150 km. in length. Shivaji Raje now controlled all Ghatmatha (range) from Sinhgad fort to Panhala fort.

On 12 November, the Marathas attacked Vasota which was one days' march by Infantry from Pratapgad. Sarvarkhan the killedar of Vasota was shocked that Shivaji Raje would start capturing the Adilshahi territory on the very next day. Shivaji Raje moved ahead leaving Kanhoji to negotiate the surrender of the fort. Sarvarkhan was the havaldar of the Panhala area and since he was besieged, forts like Panhala and Khelna fell easily.

As per Jedhe Shakavali, Panhala was captured on 28th November, i.e. seventeen days after the death of Afzalkhan.

On 28th November 1659 ie seventeen days after the elimination of Afzal Khan the Marathas reached Panhala Fort which was 225 km away from Pratapgad and besieged it. During this period we have seen that the Marathas had already captured fourteen forts. The Adilshahi garrison in Panhalgad fired cannon balls, rockets and threw huge boulders at the besiegers. The Marathas retaliated, scaled the fort and captured it after a brief skirmish When Shivaji Raje came to know of this victory he was eager to inspect the fort. He reached Panhalgad on the night of 2 December 1659. He was so keen to see this massive fort that he inspected it by torch light. By 15th February 1660, the Marathas had also captured the Khelna (Vishalgad) fort. In the next few months, both these forts would play a major role in Maratha history.

Netoji's March.

The Shivbharat 25/4-9 states that Netoji started attacking the Adilshahi kigdom. He swiftly took Kawthe, Borgaon, Kundal, Dhogaon, Sattikir, Miraj, Gokak, Dodwad, Murbad, Dharwad Kshudravaidanpur, Shamgram, Mail, Pargaon, Sangli, Kanad, Kurundwad, Kagal, Hebal, Hunnewali, Hunwad, Raibag, Hukkeri, Kadgaon, Haldi, Dhunika, Kini, Arag, Telsang, Kerur Ayug, Kamlapur, Athni, and Tikote.

The Marathas descended into the Konkan (November 1659-January 1660).

After the death of Afzal Khan, the Marathas descended from the hills of the Sahyadries into the Konkan, and Shivaji Raje literally saw the sea for the first time. He sent Doroji to seize the coastal towns including the Ports of Dabhol and Rajapur. Afzal Khan had brought with him three galbats filled with goods and treasures to Dabhol. The Bijapuri governor of Rajapur, Abdul Karim took refuge in these galbats and escaped to Jaitapur. The Marathas under Doroji chased after them to Jaitapur. Here the governor also asked the English factor, Henry Revington to take possession of the remaining three galbats.

He prepared documents claiming one of them to be English.

However he advised the other two galbats to go to the Mughal port at Surat.

The Marathas demanded that the goods in the galbat whose papers had been forged by Revington should be handed over to them. Revington agreed to do so.

The remaining two galbats which were in possession of the Adishahi were towed and anchored beyond the range of a gunshot. This enraged Doroji and knowing that this game was being played with the help of the English, he arrested the broker of the English, named Valji.

Revington then sent Giffard to negotiate with the Marathas. He too was arrested by Doroji and along with the broker Valji was jailed first in the fort at Kharepatan and then at Satavli. They remained in captivity for almost a month and were then released.

During these incursions in South Konkan, the Marathas approached Vengurla and other places bordering on Goa.

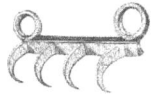

CHAPTER SEVEN

Battle of Kolhapur.

After the death of Afzalkhan and the capture of Panhala, the Adilshah in his farman dated 22nd November, ordered Rustam-i Zaman to march against Shivaji Raje. Having learnt that an Adilshahi army was marching against him, Shivaji Raje left a garrison to defend Panhala and marched out to confront the enemy. The opposing armies met near Kolhapur on 28th December 1659.

The Shivbharat Ch 24/30-70 gives a detailed description of this battle. He states, *"Hearing that Shivaji had also captured the fort of Panhala, Ali Adilshah requested the assistance of the Mughal Empire in putting down Shivaji. He also sent a strong army toward Panhala against Shivaji. This army was led by Rustam Zaman. Fazal Khan, the son of Afzal Khan, Mua Yahiya, Santaji Ghorpade, Sarjerao Ghatge were deputed to serve under him."*

Shivbharat notes the following as Shivaji Raje's officers present in the army at the time of the time of the battle. Netaji Palkar, Bhimaji Wagh, Hiraji Ingle, Mahadik, Sidhoji Pawar, Godaji Jagatap, Kharate, Pandhre, Siddi Hilal Jadhav, and Kharate's son Hanumantrao.

Shivbharat also describes the plan of battle as follows.

Rustan Zaman took his stand in the centre of his army, Fazal Khan was posted to the left wing. The right wing was guarded by Malik Itibar with his Sayyads, the rear was brought up by Fatehkhan, son of Aziz khan, and Mulla Yahia. While Santaji Ghorpade, Sarjerao Ghatge and other officers were to hover round and protect the army.

On Shivaji Raje 's side instructions issued were as follows. *"Netaji was to attack Fazalkhan. Bhimajiwagh was to attack Mulla Yahia. The Ingles were asked to march against Malik Itibar, the Mahadiks were to fight against Fateh khan, Sidhoji Pawar was to take on the Sayyads, Godaji Jagtap was to fall upon the Ghatges and Ghorpades. Shivaji Raje himself would assault against Rustum Zaman, the Kharades and Pandhres were to tackle the right wing of the enemy, while Hilal and the Jadhav would assail the left wing."*

The battle seems to have been sharp and swift. The Bijapuri force fled from the battlefield.

The booty included 12 elephants and 2,000 horses. None of the sources mentions the numerical strength of the opposing armies, but the number of elephants and horses captured by Shivaji Raje suggests that Rustam-i Zaman's army must have comprised at least 10,000 horsemen and Shivaji Raje's army must have been at least as strong and probably stronger.

It is also possible that Rustam Zaman was lukewarm in fighting against Shivaji Raje.

Shaista Khan's Mughal Army Invade Deccan.

Inspite of the outwardly show of diplomacy ie the letter written by Aurangzeb to Shivaji Raje, Aurangzeb was clear in his communication to Naziri Khan where he addresses Shivaji Raje as *son of a dog* and asks them to restrict Shivaji Raje to the south.

On 10 May 1657, Aurangzeb had written to Naziri Khan *'the accursed Shiva(ji) should be punished for his audacity and insolence.'*

On 10 Oct 1657, he had written to Naziri Khan *"that ill-fated one must be completely uprooted. Having rebelled he should be plundered, invaded and his territory despoiled. If he steps forward for a conflict, deflate his ego with your sword and punish him suitably."*

Aurangzeb was involved in the war of succession from 15 April 1658 ie battle of Dharmat to 5 June 1660 when he was coronated.

On 8 June 1658, Shah Jahan was imprisoned at Agra.

On 25 June 1658. Murad was imprisoned at the state prison of Gwalior and later killed.

On 5 January 1659, Shuja was defeated at Khajwa and exiled to Arracan (Burma)

Fig 7/1 Shaista Khan

On 13 March 1659, Dara was defeated at Deorai and later executed.

On 5 June 1659, after he had got rid of all the contenders to the throne, the grand coronation of Aurangzeb took place.

By then Aurangzeb had heard of the debacle of the Adilshahi general Afzal Khan on 10 November 1659. The Adilshah shaken by the capture of Panhala by Shivaji Raje petitioned Aurangzeb to intervene.

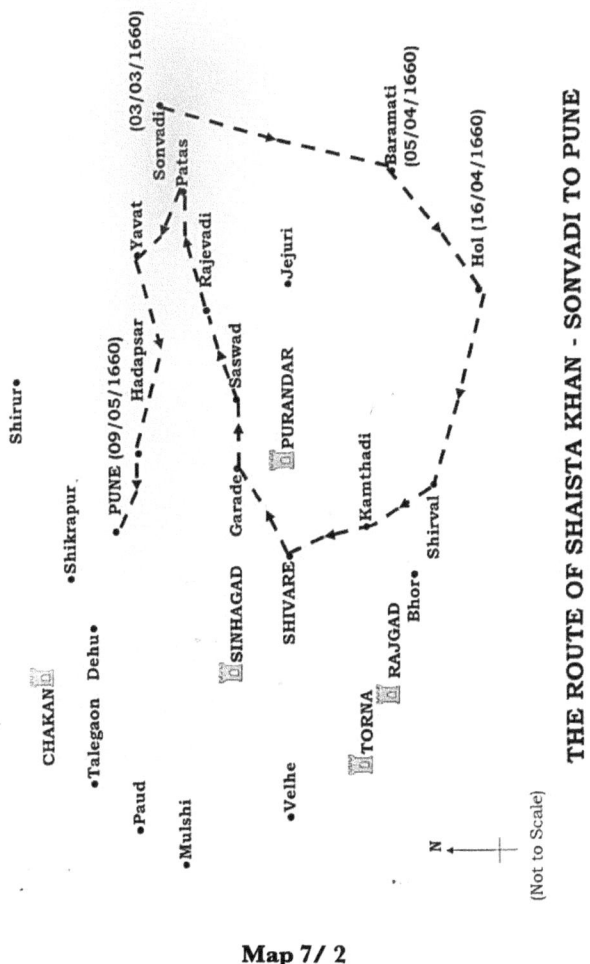

Map 7/ 2

Aurangzeb now decided to invade the Deccan and he appointed his uncle Shaista Khan as the new viceroy of the Deccan in place of Prince Muhammad Muazzam. On 28 January 1660 Shaista Khan reached Aurangabad.

The Mughal Emperor had not forgotten Shivaji Raje's foray into the Mughal dominions of Konkan.

The Shivbharat in Chap 25/57-59 states: In January 1660 Shaista Khan arrived near the Bhima River which formed the boundary of the Maratha territory. His army comprised 77,000 cavalry, excellent Buxar infantry and elephants. Shaista Khan set out from Aurangabad, the provincial capital, on 28th January 1660 with this vast army and reached Ahmednagar, 105 km to the southwest, on 11th February. He left from there on 25th February 1660, crossed the Bhima which formed the southern boundary of the Empire on 29th February and reached Sonavadi on 3rd March 1660. From Sonavadi, Shayista Khan marched to Baramati in the Supe Pargana on 5th April 1660.

The Mughal army destroyed temples, demolished monasteries, razed the houses of the principal men to the ground, cut down trees in gardens and laid waste many ancient villages and towns. Thus the country bore the appearance of the moon in total eclipse."

Marathas attack suburbs of Bijapur -Mid April 1660.

While Siddi Jauhar was approaching Panhala Shivaji Raje, to divert him sent troops towards the city of Bijapur and attacked at night its suburb called Shahapur and took it into possession after some feeble resistance and freely plundered it.

It is described in a Dutch letter dated 5th May 1660 from Vengurle thus:

"Shivaji Raje seeing that Siddi Jauhar had arrived quite near to the fort of Panhala, to which he had retired as a place of refuge, speedily dispatched four or five thousand cavalry from his army by another route to Bijapur, which, within an incredibly short time attacked at night unexpectedly the suburb of Bijapur called Shahpur and took it into possession after some feeble resistance and freely plundered it, which caused an unusual terror at the royal Court. But as it was learnt that the enemy was not strong, the Adilshah sent his bodyguard

consisting of 5,000 cavalry, which was the whole army that was left in Bijapur, under the command of Khawas Khan, the feudal lord of Vengurle, against the cavalry of Shivaji Raje. The armies struggled very long and it was doubtful which party would be successful. But the men of His majesty [i.e. the Adilshah] achieved so much that Shivaji Raje's people finally retreated six miles not without a great loss. The Siddi general [i.e. Siddi Jauhar] when he was informed of the surprise attack, sent to Bijapur 4,000 to 5,000 cavalry for the safety of Ali Adilshah."

The armies struggled very long and at last the Marathas had to retreat. Bijapur was saved, but the Adil Shahi was shocked that the Marathas had come up to their doorstep.

Ali Adilshah regarded Shivaji Raje's retreat as a great victory, as is evidenced by the following farman that Ali Adilshah sent to Ekoji Bhosale on 3 March 1660.

"As our aim is to spread the religion of the Chief of the Prophets [i.e.Muhammad] we are always blessed with victory. For instance, as the infidel (kafir) rebel, Shivaji Raje, has raised rebellion we have sent Siddi Jauhar Salabat Khan at the head of our army to extirpate him. When the Khan marched out, Shivaji Raje, unable to fight against him, took to flight and his army of disbelievers was scattered. Now the army of Islam is pursuing him and will, in a short time, either make him a captive or annihilate him. On hearing these glad tidings offer thanks for our good fortune."

Siddi Jauhar - the Lion of Kurnool.

Siddi Jauhar was an Abyssinian Muslim who held a jagir at Kurnool, about 260 km east-southeast of Bijapur.

After the death of Mohamad Shah, Siddi Jauhar had refused to recognize the new sovereign ie Ali Adilshah presumebly because he was the illegitimate son born of one of the women from Ali 's harem. He had been brought up by the queen Badi Begamsahiba and later placed him on the throne. In this way she wielded power behind the throne.

With the death of Afzalkhan, Siddi Jauhar decided to make amends. He petitioned to Ali Adilshah saying he was apologetic for his past behavior and was willing subjugate Shivaji Raje.

Ali Adilshah had no alternative but to forgive his past crimes and to give him the title of Salabat Khan (indestructible) and send him against Shivaji Raje. The Adilshahi organized a new army in three months and put it under his command. The army given under his command comprised, according to a dispatch dated 5th May 1660 by the Dutch resident at Vengurle, 35 to 40 thousand infantry and 16 to 20 thousand cavalry. The principal noblemen in the army included Rustam-i Zaman, Jauhar's son-in-law Siddi Masud, Afzal Khan's eldest son Fazil Khan, commander of the infantry Bade Khan, Sadat Khan, Bhai Khan (son of Wali Khan), Baji Ghorpade and Pid Naik.

Siddi Johar started from Kurnool and came via Athani-Miraj and straight away proceeded to Panhala.

From the middle of Jan 1660 to middle of Feb 1660 Shivaji Raje had laid siege of Miraj. When Shivaji Raje came to know of this development, he lifted the siege of Miraj and took charge of Panhalgad by the end of Feb 1660.

On 02 Mar 1660, Siddi Johar laid siege of Panhalgad while Rustum Jemah and Fazal khan besieged Khelna (Vishalgad.)

Unlike Afzal Khan, Siddi Johar was neither cruel, nor treacherous nor a megalomaniac. He was a straight and simple fighter . He was very good at strategy, therefore he was accompanied by Baji Timaji Deshpande who was a strategist with the title of Diyanat Rao.

During this time it is pertinent to note that Shivaji Raje had to keep his one eye on the Mughals.

On 03 Mar 1660, Shaista Khan arrived in Deccan at Pune.

On 21 Jun 1660, Shaista Khan besieged Chakan.

Siddi Johar traps Shivaji Raje in Panhala.

At first, Shivaji Raje was not too worried of the siege of Panhala as he knew that :

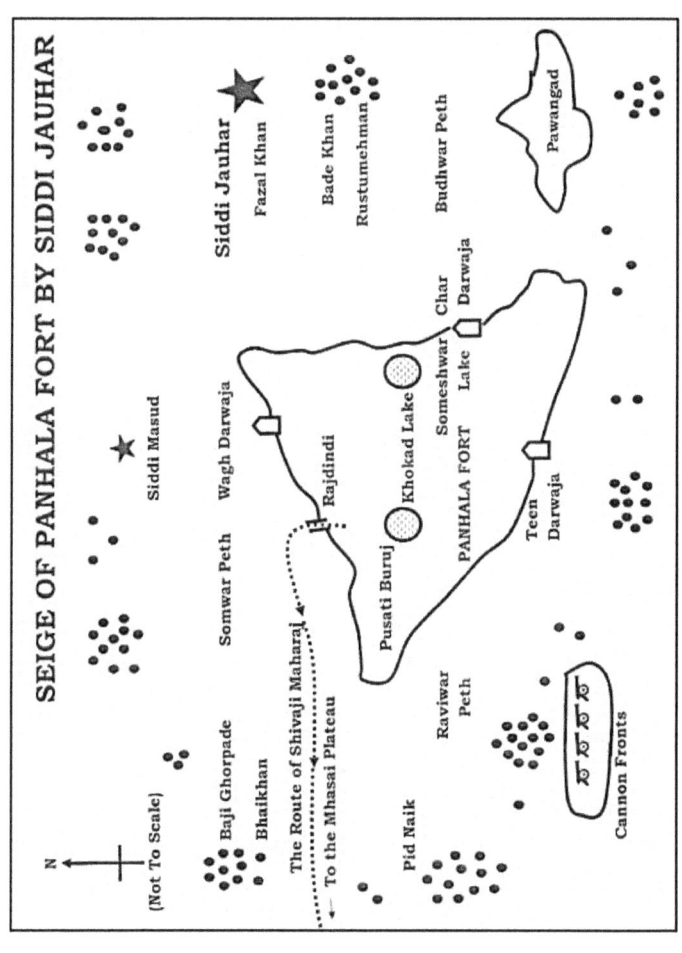

Map 7/ 3

1-No siege in the Sahyadry was impenetrable. Panhala is perched on an immense mountain-mass covered with thick vegetation, strewn with boulders and cut by brooks and ravines. There were granaries with enough stocks to last six months. The periphery of the fortifications on the summit is about seven kilometers and that of the mountain mass at its base is much greater. The siege therefore could not be an unbroken cordon but was rather a chain of outposts established below the mountain. Siddi Jauhar would be compelled to raise the siege at the approach of the rainy season which was drawing near.

2-Netoji Palkar was out side and Shivaji Raje was confident that he could break any siege.

On 5th June 1660 Henry Revington, the Chief of the English trading station at Rajapur, wrote that *Shivaji Raje was besieged in Panhala with 8,000 infantry and 60 horsemen.*

A Dutch letter, from Vengurle describes the siege of Panhala, *"In the meanwhile Shivaji Raje's people appeared now and again with a flying army about Bijapur and tried unsuccessful attempts to decoy Siddi Jauhar from his camp, but they had to flee with some loss every time they tried to do so."* On 17th April 1660, they wrote to Revington who had reached Panhala: *"We should be very glad that Shivaji Raje's forces that were at Bijapur were gone towards home, as is reported, so that there might be the more hopes of gaining that castle out of his hands."*

Netoji's futile attempts to raise the siege of Panhala are described in the Shivabharat Chap 26/1-25 thus: *"When Netoji returned to Rajgad, Shivaji Raje's mother Jijabai reproved him for having returned out of fear of the enemy, leaving his master in the beleaguered fortress and declared her resolve to go herself to the rescue of her only son. Netoji dissuaded her from her determination and himself set out towards Panhala. When Jauhar learnt of the enemy's approach he dispatched a part of his army to intercept them. In the ensuing battle Netaji Palkar's relieving force was routed and Siddi Yahya, son of Siddi Hilal, was wounded, unhorsed and taken prisoner."*

RAINFALL IN PANHALA

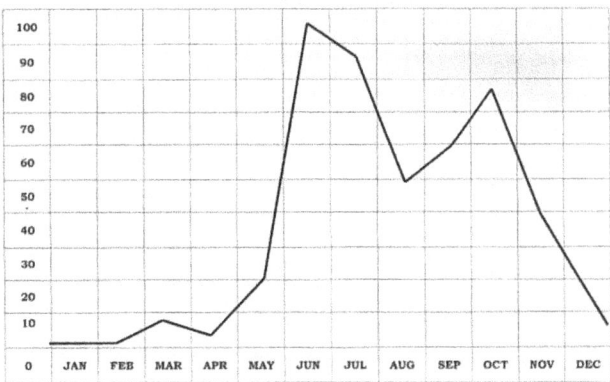

Fig 7/ 4

2 April to 5 June 1660 -The Revington Affair.

Shivaji Raje never had cannons or elephants in his army. His army was swift and he himself called his soilders *parinda* .(birds)

But he was always short of cannons for his forts and ships.

Revington was the the Chief of the English trading station at Rajapur.

Though all foreigners were supposed to be neutral during times of war, Revington decided to break this rule. After seeing that the Adilshahi forces could not break the siege at Panhala he decided to sell cannons and granado shells to Siddi Jauhar.

He went a step further and volunteered to fire the guns himself.

On 2nd April 1660, Revington with two of his colleagues - Philip Giffard and William Mingham set out with one mortar and fifty "granado shells" to give an on-site demonstration. These English cannons were fired between 15 May and 5 June 1660, Richard Taylor, Rowland Garway and Richard Napier were with them at Panhalgad.

Battle Of Chakan June-Aug 1661.

After the capture of Supe on 05 April 1660, Shaista Khan captured Shirval and attacked the area around Rajgad and went to Pune. (Map 7/2)

Shaista khan decided to pass the monsoon of 1660 in the Pune region. However the Marathas had anticipated his move and razed the area, so there was no food or fodder for his vast army. He then decided to shift his base to Chakan which was a fort 25 km north of Pune.

Supplies at Chakan were easier as it was well connected and was midway between the Konkan -Bhor ghat -Ahmednagar route.

Unlike most of the forts in the Sahyadries which were hill forts, Sangram Durga of Chakan was a land fort. It was squarish and had high walls with bastions and towers at four corners. Round the walls was a ditch about 30 feet deep and fifteen feet wide.

Shaista Khan started the siege from 21 June and with his supreme confidence in Mughal siege technology he expected the garrison to capitulate in 10-15 days.

Firangoji Narsala the killedar was an old man in his sixties and a contemporary of Shahaji Raje.

On 23 June 1660, the Mughals attacked the fort with 20,000 soldiers.

Firangoji Narasala knew he was hopelessly outnumbered, he had only 320 soldiers. In keeping with the policy of '*no unnecessary suicidal war*', Shivaji Raje had asked his commander to leave the fort.

However, Firangoji decided not to abandon the fort and instead started an impossible war against the Mughals. Shocked troops from both sides watched as he counter attacked and defended the fort in this way for 56 days.

As a last resort the Mughals dug a tunnel up to the fort; which was a challenge because of the June monsoons. They managed to fill this tunnel with explosives and blew up the wall of the fort. This was a major setback for Firangoji and his mavla-soldiers; 75 soldiers died in this attack. The Mughal army rushed into the fort; fierce fighting ensued and many Maratha soldiers were killed.

As we saw during this time (03 Mar - 13 July 1660) Shivaji Raje was besieged at Panhgalgad, and it was here that he heard about the bravery of Firangoji.

The Chakan siege ended on 14 August 1660.

But Shaista Khan was astonished by Firangoji's bravery, and offered him a Mughal *Mansabdari*. Needless to say, Firangoji refused to accept it. Respecting his gallantry, Shaista Khan gave him and his soldier's safe passage.

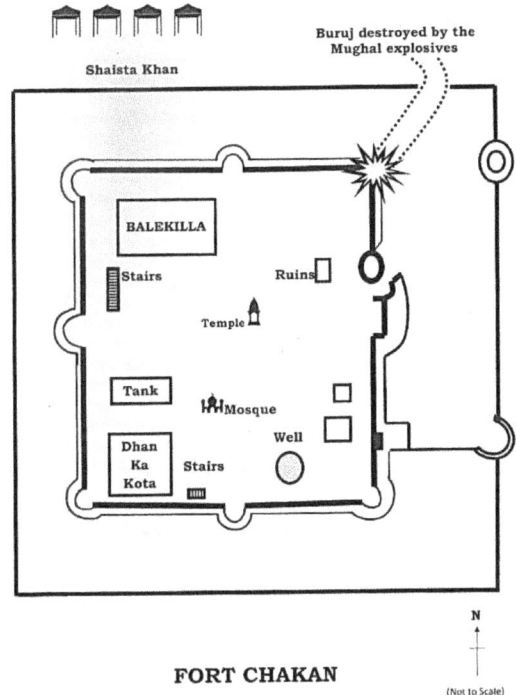

FORT CHAKAN

(Not to Scale)

Map 7/ 5

The battle of Chakan is important because, it heralds the first proper invasion and victory by the Mughals against the Marathas after Aurangzeb sent Shaista Khan to the Deccan.

Shivaji Raje makes a daring plan.

In his letter dated 27th July 1660, the Dutch Resident at Vengurle remarks that Shivaji Raje's idea in going to Panhala was that the onset of monsoons that was drawing near would force Jauhar to raise the siege. (Fig 7/ 3)

However, despite the commencement of the rainy season, Siddi Johar showed no inclination to do so. The same letter tells us that the Adilshahi commander erected hovels to shelter his men and pressed on with the siege.

The resident also mentions 'strong rumours' that there was a shortage of provisions in the Panhala fort.

Still worse, Revington with fifty "granado shells" had bombarded Panhala.

With no possibility of Netoji breaking the siege, Shivaji Raje knew that he himself had to find a way out. And a daring plan was formed.

Shivaji Raje expected the siege of Panhala to last till the onset of the monsoon. But Siddi Johar tenaciously tightened the siege.

Shivbharat says: that the Devi Tuljabhavani appeared in Shivaji Raje's dreams and extolled him to escape from Panhalgad, now that Moghuls had captured Fort Chakan.

She commanded -You cannot fight both the Adishahi and the Mughals. Leave with a few soldiers, the garrison at Panhalgad will fight on their own.

In first week of July, Shivaji Raje sent an envoy named Gangadhar Pant with a message to Siddi Johar that he was willing to meet the Adilshahi commander personally and deliver all his possessions if

Siddi Johar promised to pardon him for his past offences and protect him as would a father.

The proposal had its effect and the Adilshahi soldiers who were on their toes, till now, relaxed their vigilance.

Shivaji Raje appointed Trimbak Bhaskar as the (killedar) commandant of the fort before setting out.

Maharaj Escapes from Panhala (13 July 1660).

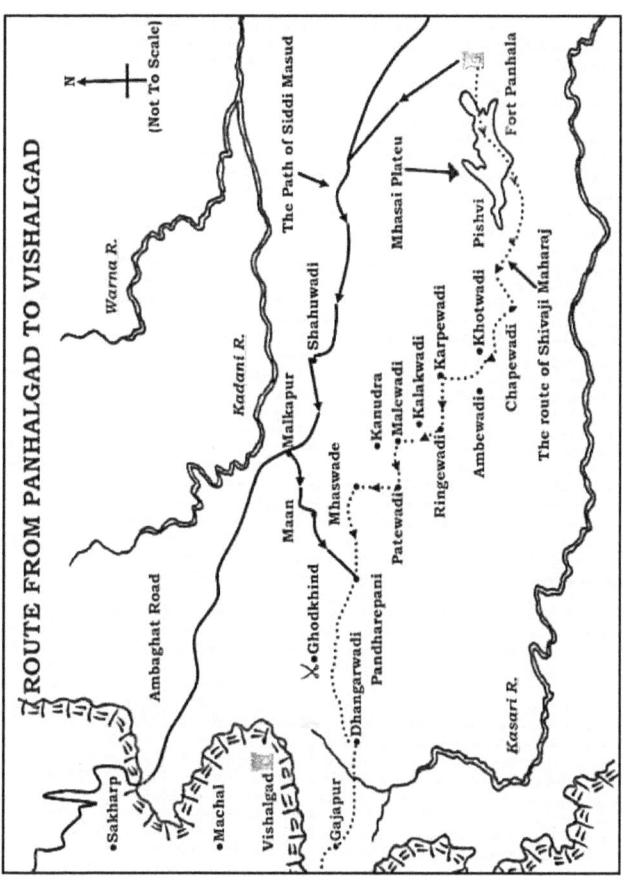

Map 7/ 6

In the first quarter of the following night, i.e. 13th July 1660, a palanquin left the fort with the usual pomp and glory associated with Shivaji Raje. It reached the tent of Siddi Jauhar and Shivaji Raje was given a warm welcome. Just as Siddi Jauhar was admiring his prize captive, Fazal Khan the son of the dead Afzal Khan entered the tent and one look at the captive told him that this was not the real Shivaji Raje but an imposter. This is because Fazal had seen Shivaji Raje at close quarters after the death of his father Afzal Khan. It must be remembered that Fazal Khan was brought to Shivaji Raje as a prisoner and Shivaji Raje could have easily killed him. But Shivaji Raje allowed him safe passage. Instead of being grateful to Shivaji Raje, at the first opportunity he came to Panhalgad lusting for revenge.

To Siddi Johar's utter astonishment the captured king turned out to be a barber, named Shiva Kashid.

A furious Siddi Johar put the barber to death immediately. But he died a contented death. Legend says that when he was first told of this plan where he have to masquerade as Shivaji Raje, his happiness knew no bounds. He had no qualms that he was going to a sure death. He was ecstatic that while dying he would be wearing clothes worn by his king .

A detailed analysis of Shiva Kashid will be done later in chapter eight ie Analysis of the Pratapgad War.

Siddi Johar 's heart sank in bitter disappointment as all the exertions and vigilance of the past three or four months had proved in vain. His prey had escaped, *like a jewel spilt from a bag.*

The Bandals and the Battle of Ghod Khind

In the meanwhile, another palanquin with Shivaji Raje in it had sneaked out of the fort under cover of darkness aided by stormy weather and torrents of rain. He was accompanied by 600 Bandals led by Baji Prabhu Deshpande. The party slipped out of the besiegers' lines and headed for Vishalgad.

However, the enemy scouts saw the escaping *palkhi* and reported it to Siddi Johar. Johar kept his head and reasoned that all was not lost. After all it was pouring and the ground was slushy and slippery. The rivers were in spate and the path was tortuous.

Siddi Jauhar pulled himself together and dispatched a pursuing force, comprising 1000 infantry and 2000 cavalry, under his son-in-law Siddi Masud. The heroic sacrifice of Shiva Kashid gave the fleeing Maratha force enough time for Shivaji Raje to reach a strategic location ie Ghodkhind (Horse Pass), a gorge. It was very narrow so that only a few soldiers could pass abreast. Baji Prabhu Deshpande, a gallant sardar along with 300 of his Bandal sena, took the position to defend the pass till Shivaji Raje reached another fort, Vishalgad.

Battle of Pawankhind was a rear-guard battle and a Last Stand that took place on 13 July 1660 at a mountain pass in the vicinity of fort Vishalgad. The Adilshahi forces were 1000 infantry and 2000 cavalry against 300 Maratha light infantry. Baji Prabhu and his brother Fulaji successfully defended the pass with 300 soldiers. They were fatally wounded and the mercenary soldiers of Siddi Masood were taken-aback by the macabre sight of those 300 soldiers bleeding heavily but fighting brutally with dandpattas (long swords) in both hands . They continued fighting and stopped only when they heard the sound of three cannons shots fired by Shivaji Raje from the Vishalgad fort, indicating that he had reached safely. After crossing the pass Shivaji Raje had to cross a small rivulet called Kasari, but this rivulet due to the torrential rains had swelled into a raging, virulent river. Shivaji Raje swam through this river only to meet another obstacle in their route to Vishalgad.

Unknown to Shivaji Raje on the north east side of Panhalgad, Suryaji Surve and Jaswant Dalvi were camping between Panhalgad and Vishalgad to counter any possibility of the garrison from Vishalgad reaching Panhalgad. Now Shivaji Raje and his 300 Bandal soldiers though tired after the escape took on the enemy.

However Rango Narayan Sarpotdar, Shivaji Raje's young officer on the Vishalgad Fort took stock of the situation, and repulsed the Surves and the Dalvis with heavy losses.

The pass is now known as *Pävan Khind*– (The Sacred Pass).

The *talwarichya panacha man* (sword of honour) which was with the Jedhes after the Pratapgad battle was now given to the Bandals. Baji's eldest son was offered a job as chief of a section. His other seven sons were given the *honour of the Palkhi*.

Fig 7/ 7 Baji Prabhu at Pawankhind

The Battle off Pavankhind was the last major battle between Adilshahi forces and Marathas. Hereafter Marathas were recognized as an independent power.

War is about fighting and killing and being killed but this was the first instance of the Mavlas willing to accept sure death. The sacrifice of Baji Prabhu Deshpande and Shiva Kashid is a legend in itself and will be discussed later, in chapter eight ie Analysis .

The Jedhe Chronology says thus:

"*13th July 1660: His Highness [i.e. Shivaji Raje] came down from Panhala and went to Khelna [i.e. Vishalgad]. Siddi Jauhar's army came in pursuit. A great melee occurred during which Bandal's men fought valorously. Men perished. Baji Prabhu, the Deshkulkarni [of Hirdas Maval], was killed.*"

Battle Of Umberkhind 1661. (Map 7/8)

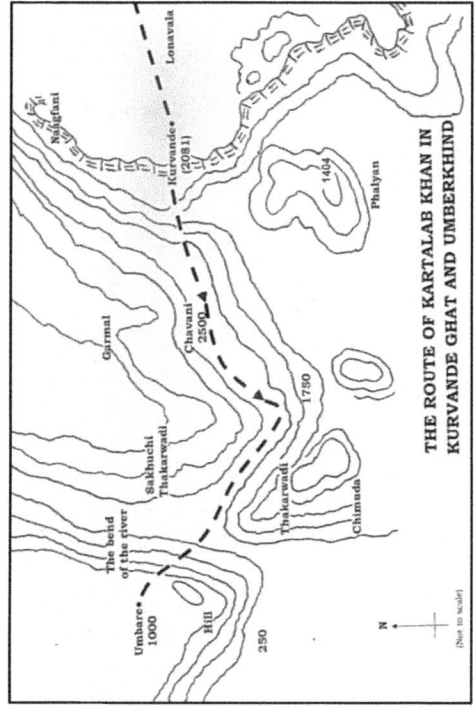

On 15 Aug 1661, we saw that Chakan surrendered after 56 days of unparalleled fight. Shaista Khan decided not to try and take any of Shivaji Raje's forts. He decided to torch, plunder and devastate the Maratha country-side.

The Shivbharat states in Ch 28/59-53 that on 03 Feb 1661, *"Shaista Khan sent Kartalab Khan an Uzbek along with Rai Bagan to capture North Konkan i.e. Nagothane, Chaul, Panvel, Kalyan and Bhivandi. Under his command he sent Kacchap, Chavan, Amarsingh, Mitrasen, Sarjerao Gadhe and Jaswant Kokate. He was also accompanied by Rai Bagan (Royal Tigress), the wife of Deshmukh of Mahur Sarkar of Berar, Raje Udaram. Kartalab Khan marched from Pune via Lohgad through the narrow broken roads of Kurwande pass (15 km east of Pen and six km east of Umbare village)*

We have already discussed that Shivaji Raje had a well organized intelligence system. He also paid well for accurate and timely reports.

Shivaji Raje came to know about this movement from his spies and he laid a trap at Umberkhind. At Umberkhind, the foot track is very narrow like the barrel of a gun. On all four sides the gorge is shut by hills as seen in Map 7/8.

When the Mughals entered Umberkhind, the stillness of the forest was broken by the ominous beatings of the Maratha war drums. The whole Mughal army was stunned. Then the Marathas attacked the Mughal army with arrows and sling shots. Kartalab Khan and Rai Bagan with other Mughal soldiers tried to retaliate, but the forest was so dense and Maratha army was so quick that the Mughals could not even see the enemy. The situation was such that Mughal soldiers seemed to be fighting ghosts. As if this was not all, the terrain left no room to hide, deploy, retreat or rally.

Rai Bagan then convinced Kartalab Khan, that he had led his army into a death trap. He had no option but to surrender and ask for mercy. She said, *"You have made a mistake by putting the whole army in the jaws of a lion. Shivaji Raje is the lion. You should not have chosen this path to attack Shivaji Raje Now, to save your soldiers from being slaughtered, you should surrender yourself to Shivaji Raje. Unlike Mughals, Shivaji Raje shows mercy to those who surrender."* Kartalab was speechless, because he had just been made a char hazariat after the bravery he had shown at the battle of Dharmat (15 April 1658) which was a part of the Mughal war of succession.

The Umberkhind battle lasted for hardly two hours. And then Kartalab Khan sent out the truce party under Nazar Inayat. They shouted *"truce, truce!"* and within a minute got encircled by Shivaji Raje's men.

The Shivbharat Ch 29 /15-25 says that *Shivaji Raje himself was leading this ambush. Kartalab and his officers saw him astride a bejeweled horse in the way of Vishnu on his Eagle, a regal figure in armor, a sequined crest on his forehead, long neck, broad chest, muscular arms, with two quivers on each side like the wings of a bird, two long swords hung from his gold embroidered belt, his face though outwardly calm masked a ferocious look, in his right hand was along spear. He looked more fierce than Lord Shankar, more unbearable than fire, more forceful than the wind, more richer than Kuber, more powerful than Lord Indra, more cruel than Yama, more in conquerable than Madan, more pleasant than the moon.*

Then on the condition of paying huge ransom and surrendering all the arms, Kartalab Khan was allowed to go back free.

The battle of Umberkhind stunned all the Muslims because a miniscule Maratha army of 3000 had brought a huge Mughal army of 30,000 to its knees. What was significant is that Shivaji Raje led this army himself.

The victory in this battle again shows that Shivaji Raje's spies had brought the news of Kartalab Khan route from Lonavala to Pen and the date and the strength of his army.

The victory also shows that Shivaji Raje had a through knowledge of the exact point when the route from Chavni to Thakarwadi narrows

Fig 7/9

like the barrel of a gun. At the same time the surrounding hills and dense jungles made it impossible to see the Marathas leave alone to fight them.

The battle of Chakan (1660) and the battle of Umerkhind (1661) terrified Shaista Khan. After that his armies went about ravaging and plundering the land. However, Shiasta Khan refused to get involved in any direct action.

Lightening strike on Shaista Khan at Lal Mahal.

We have already seen in Chapter one that during his teenage years Shivaje Raje had lived in a palace called Lal Mahal. Later he built and shifted his residence to Rajgad. From 09 May 1660 onwards Shaista Khan was occupying Shivaji Raje's Lal Mahal. Shaista Khan's harem was with him. Surrounding him were his eunuchs, guards, attendants, band room offices and beyond that an army of almost one lakh. On the other side of his camp was Jaswant Singh with an army of 10,000.

After the fiasco at Chakan and the debacle at Umber khind, Shaista Khan had decided on a policy of wait and watch. He made no heroic attempts. Instead, he ravaged the land of crops and burnt homes. Shivaji Raje had no option but to oust him out of Swarajya.

The day chosen was the 6th day of Ramzan.

On 4/5 Apr 1663, it was the birthday of Badshah Aurangzeb. A group of Marathas planted by Shivaji Raje obtained special permission for a wedding procession. Nearly 200 men led by Shivaji Raje disguised as the bridegroom's procession members entered the Lal Mahal at Pune. Another 200 led by Bapuji Babuji and Chimnaji Bapuji entered in small parties dressed as laborers and soldiers of Maratha generals serving under Shaista Khan.

After the midnight of 4 April 1663, the Marathas raided the compound and entered the palace through the kitchen. Some cooks had woken to prepare the pre-dawn meal. They were quickly killed. The raiders made a small opening in the wall and entered the harem. Like all Mughal harems, the place was a maze of lace, screen wall after screen wall and enclosure within enclosure. Shivaji Raje and his group hacked away through them and soon reached the bedroom of Shaista Khan. But the noise alerted some maid servants. They realized that something was amiss and in spite of their fright did two things. They extinguished the lights and woke up Shaista Khan.

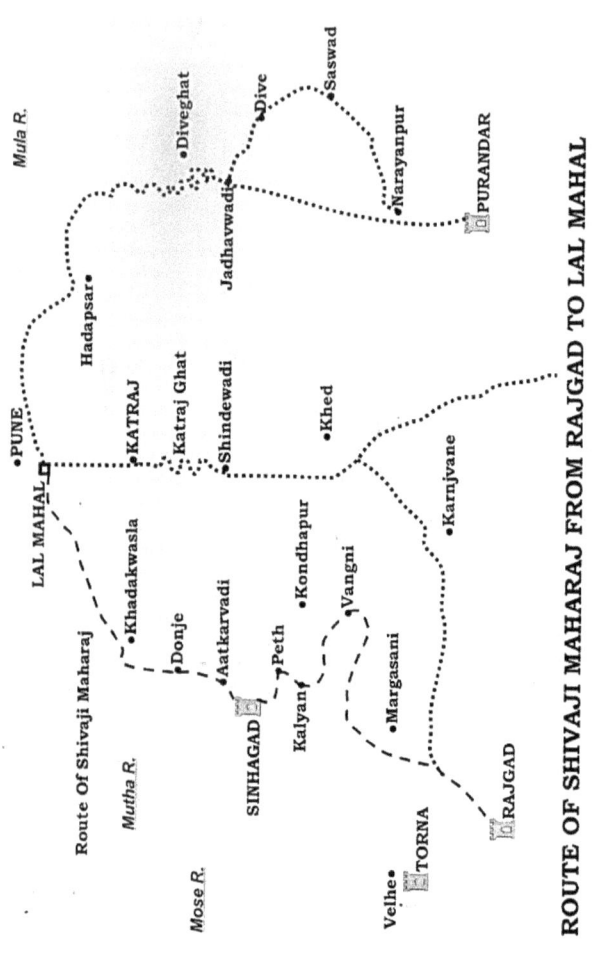

Map 7/ 10

A skirmish followed in the harem. As if this shock and awe was not enough, two of the Marathas fell into a cistern of water. This added bewilderment to the shrieks and screams of the women, some of whom had never even seen an unknown male. In the melee Shaista Khan lost three fingers, while his son Abul Fath and his son in law were killed. Along with them, another 40-50 men were also killed.

In this encounter the woman body guards and eunuchs fought well and 12 were killed. Taking advantage of the confusion and darkness, the Marathas escaped from the palace and reached Sinhgad. Six Marathas were killed and forty were wounded.

This night attack was a complete success. The retreat from the palace was unmolested. No one pursued the attackers.

Since Shivaji Raje led the attack in person, to the Marathas he became a living romantic legend. To the Mughals he was a reincarnation of Satan. No place was safe from him. Not even harems. No feat was impossible for him. There was a mixture of humiliation, terror and sorrow in the Mughal camp.

On 14 May 1663, Aurangzeb came to know of this dare devil raid while on his way from Lahore to Kashmir. He angrily transferred Shaista Khan to Bengal and refused to meet him.

Thus the Pratapgad War started with the appointment of Afzalkhan in March 1659 ended in May 1663 with the transfer of Shaista Khan to Bengal.

Afzal Khan was killed on Shrinrupshalivahan Shake 1581 wikari naam Samwatsari, Margashish Shudh Saptamis , guruwari 8 we tasi (10 November 1659 at 2.00 pm). This date according to the Hindu calender is celebrated as Shivpratap Diwas.

CHAPTER EIGHT

Analysis of The Pratapgad War

The Pratapgad War was a tripartite war. It was started by Aurangzeb when he extoled the Adilshahi to subdugate Shivaji Raje.

a- Shivaji Raje and San Zu

San Tzu has said: *1-'All warfare is based on deception. The army should not be only physically strong it should also be mentally strong i.e., espirite de corps.*
We saw the fledgling Maratha army was mentally tough enough to take on an army that was larger in numbers, better equipped and led by a battle hardened general.

2-When able to attack, we must seem unable; when using our forces, we must seem inactive.
We saw that the Maratha army decided to withdraw from the theatre of war from Pune area without putting up a fight.

3- when we are near, we must make the enemy believe we are far, when we are far, we must make him believe we are near.
From the time that Afzal Khan crossed Mahabaleshwar. unknown to him, the Marathas were always close to him observing his every move. But they were neither seen nor heard .

4-Hold out baits to entice the enemy and crush him. The good tactician plays with his adversary as a cat plays with a mouse.
Shivaji Raje as we saw put himself as bait. Afzal Khan fell into this trap. From almost April 1659 to 9 November 1659 Afzal Khan was the cat and Shivaji Raje was the mouse. On 10 November at about

3.00 pm Shivaji Raje became the cat and Afzal Khan became the mouse.

b-Wagh nakh, what and why?

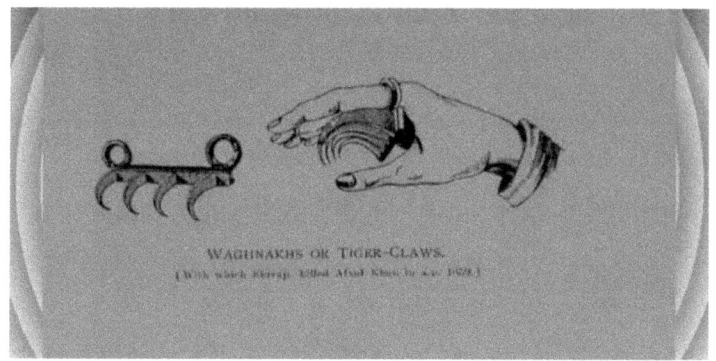

Fig 8 / 1

The story of Hiranyakashyap

The Bhagavata Purāṇa describes that Vishnu, in his previous avatar as Varāha, (boar) killed the evil asura Hiraṇayakṣa. The older brother of Hirṇayakṣa, demon king Hiraṇyakaśipu, hated Vishnu and wanted revenge. He undertook many years of austere penance to gain special powers. Thereafter, Brahma offered Hiraṇyakaśipu a boon. Hiraṇyakaśipu asked, *"Grant me that I not die within any residence or outside any residence, during the daytime or at night, nor on the ground or in the sky. Grant me that my death not be brought about by any weapon, nor by any human being or animal. Grant me that I not meet death from any entity, living or non living created by you. Grant me, further, that I not be killed by any demigod or demon or by any great snake from the lower planets."* Brahma granted him the boon, and Hiraṇyakaśipu gained these powers.

Hiraṇyakaśipu, once powerful and invincible with the new boon, began to persecute those who were devotees of Vishnu.

In order to kill Hiraṇyakasipu and not upset the boon given by Brahma, the form of Narasiṃha was chosen. Hiraṇyakasipu could not be killed by human, deva or animal. Narasiṃha was none of these, as he is a form of Viṣṇu incarnate as a part-human, part-animal. He came upon Hiraṇyakasipu at twilight (when it is neither day nor night) on the threshold of a courtyard (neither indoors nor out), and put the demon on his thighs (neither earth nor space). Using his sharp fingernails (neither animate nor inanimate) as weapons, he disembowelled and killed the demon king.

Shivaji Raje must have heard this tale from his mother Jijamata.

He must have taken inspiration from this tale to use the Wagh Nakh.

This is the first time that this small weapon was used by Shivaji Raje against a giant of a man like Afzal Khan, though it finds mention in the Rig vedas.

Shivaji Raje did not use this weapon again. Nor was it used by any other warrior later.

c- Shivaji Raje and World History.

Most kings and generals did not take part in the actual battle preferring to direct it from a nearby hillock. If they did take part, they did so astride an elephant. Shivaji Raje was the only king who led from the front astride a horse and with a sword in hand.

During the attack on Afzal Khan he put own life in peril, which made the whole of Hindustan look at him in awe. Shivaji Raje was the only king /general who had a duel with a warrior bigger than him, stronger than him and more experienced than him.

It must have taken a lot of guts to embrace Afzal khan who was instrumental in murdering his brother Sambhaji.

It was also the first time, that Shivaji Raje put his life in peril. And he was absolutely alone.

During the Agra visit he was imprisoned and Aurangzeb had decided to kill him, but he could not do so because he had come under the protection of Jaisingh.

When his son Ramsingh came to know of this, he sent word to the Bakshi *"The Emperor has decided to slay Shivaji Raje but he has come here under a guarantee of safety from my father. So, it is proper that the Emperor should first kill me, call up my son and kill him too, and after slaying us put Shiva (ji) to death or do what he likes to him."*

Similarly during the escape from Panhalgad Shivaji Raje's life was in peril but he had the 300 Bandals who formed a human defensive wall at Pawankhind. It was so impregnable that that Siddi Jauhar's army of 5000 could not breach it for a long time.

In all his life time Shivaji Raje came closest to being killed during the Afzal Khan -Shivaji Raje duel.

d-Role of Shiva Kashid at siege of Panhalgad.

Legend says that when he was first told of this plan where he have to masquerade as Shivaji Raje, his happiness knew no bounds. He had no qualms that he was going to a sure death. He was ecstatic that while dying he would be wearing clothes worn by his king and he died a contented death.

Folk tales also says, he uttered in rapture, "I was born a barbar, but I will die a king."

The sacrifice of Shiva Kashid is the core of the Swarajya that Shivaji Raje established. Let us analyse why?

Shivaji Raje was at the siege of Miraj when he came to know that Siddi Jauhar was marching towards him from the east ie Kunnur and so was Shaista Khan striding towards him and had reached Aurangabad.

In the last week of February Shivaji Raje took refuge in fort Panhala and on 02 March Siddi Jauhar laid siege to Panhala. That means Shiva Kashid saw Shivaji Raje for the first time in the beginning of March and for the last time on 12 July 1659. That is about five months

Lets presume that Shiva Kashid visited Shivaji Raje once a month for a hair cut and three more times for a weekly beard trim. That means they interacted a total of about twenty times.

In these twenty times Shiva Kashid became so enamored with Shivaji Raje and his idea of Swarajya that he was willing to die for this idea.

Mind you he was not a warrior, but a mere barber. He was not a part of the fighting tribes like the Jedhes, Bandals, Gaikwads, Ghorpades who lived to die. And to die fighting.

That makes the sacrifice Shiva Kashid all the more intriguing, astonishing and noble.

e-Role of Shivaji Raje and geography.

In his sequel to the history of Sevagy, written after his second visit to India in 1672, Carre paid a visit to Shivaji Raje's governor of Chaul who drew the best portrait (of him) in the world.

'Ever destined to conquer a part of the world, he had studied with extreme care everything about the duty of a general and that of a soldier, above all (the art of) fortification, which he understood better than the ablest engineers, and geography, of which he had made a special study, and which he had mastered and to such an extent as to know not merely all the cities including the smallest townships of the country, but even the lands and the bushes of which he had prepared very exact charts.'

Adept at making friends, like his wealth, his friends were innumerable, "they sent him information every hour. Concluding the chapter Carre remarks, I understood that valour has its rewards and that great men find praise even in the mouth of their enemies."

Shivaji Raje used the topography of the Sahyadries to entice Afzal Khan to come from the flat plains of Pune to the sky kissing peaks and abysmal valleys of Jawli.

In the same way Shivaji Raje also used his knowledge of geography to take on the 5000 strong army of Siddi Masud with only 300 Bandals only because he was aware of the bottle neck at Ghod Khind.

f- Afzal Khan's galbat and the Maratha Navy.

We have seen that Shivaji Raje family was originally from Ellora in Marathwada and his maternal family was from Sindakhedraja.

He was born at Shivneri and after spending a brief period in Bangalore he settled in the jagir of his father Shivaji Raje at Pune. He was about 12 years old. He killed Afzal Khan at the age of 29 years.

After the death of Afzal Khan, the Marathas descended from the hills of the Sahyadrys into the Konkan, and Shivaji Raje literally saw the sea for the first time.

He saw the wealth that sea trade brought and thereafter he formed the Navy.

Spies

Much of the credit of Shivaji Raje's escapades go to the spies. Chanakya says " Spies are the eyes and ears of kingdom "

San Tzu says "*Spies should be paid well for every day costs in time money and lives. So, neglecting the use of spies is nothing less than a crime against humanity. Spies are recruited from worthy men who been degraded from office, criminals who have undergone punishment, favourite concubines who are greedy for gold, men who are aggrieved at being in subordinate positions or have been passed over presents. They should never be known to anybody nor should anybody know them.*"

Shivaji Raje used spies to carry out espionage for raids on Surat, Burhanpur, Jalna and for the escape from Agra. Notable among them were Bahirji Naik who carried out espionage for Shivaji Raje and commanded a force of 3,000 but besides Bahirji the names of very few are known. The spies were made up of wandering communities like Ramoshis, Dhangers, Bhils, Kamans, Vanzara, Pardhi, Mahadeo Koli, and Masan Jogis. Shivaji Raje also used his spy network to find a way out of tricky situations like Panhalgad. The spies came from the wandering gypsy like communities and were looked down upon but, Shivaji Raje gave them the title of Naik.

When he sacked any town, he knew from his spies how much wealth each merchant had and where it was stored. He also knew who were the philanthropist and who were the cut throat businessman (see below) Shivaji Raje paid all his men well but the spies were paid the highest rate.

The spies used to converse in a hand sign language called Karpallavi.

This is quite similar to the signage used by the deaf and dumb today.

Shivaji Maharaj and Astronomy

Shivaji Maharaj was one of the most versatile persons of Medieval India.

We already know that Shivaji Maharaj was well versed in guerilla war fare, geography, climate, fort architecture, trade and commerce, maritime warfare and trade, ship building, taxation and town planning.

But we are amazed to know that he was also aware of the role of astronomy/astrology in the role of war. The following discussion and charts show that sky charts during the major events in the life of Shivaji Maharaj resembled one another.

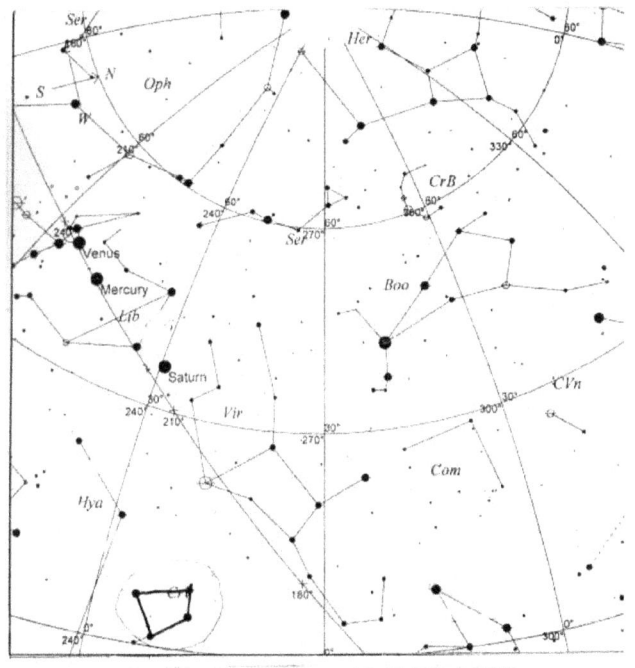

PRATAPGAD WAR - 10 NOV 1659

Fig 8/ 2

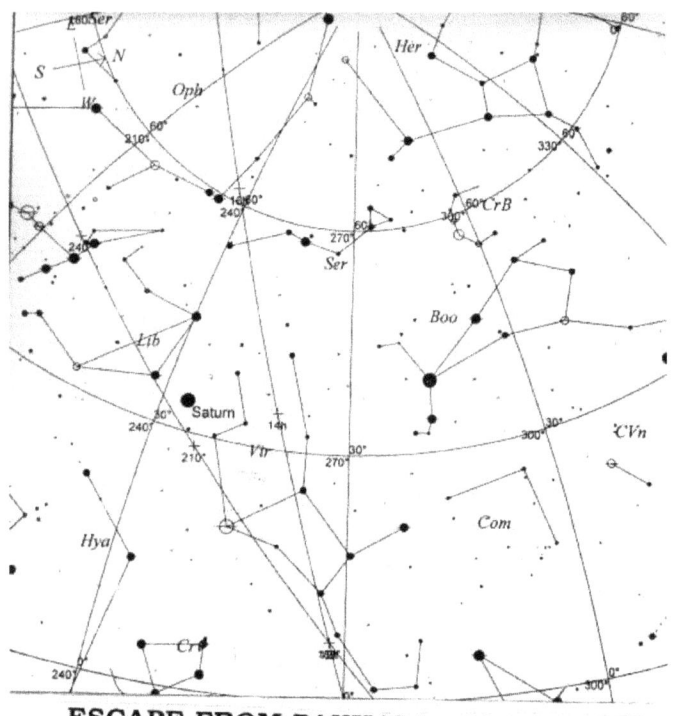

ESCAPE FROM PANHALA - 13 JUL 1660

Fig 8/ 3

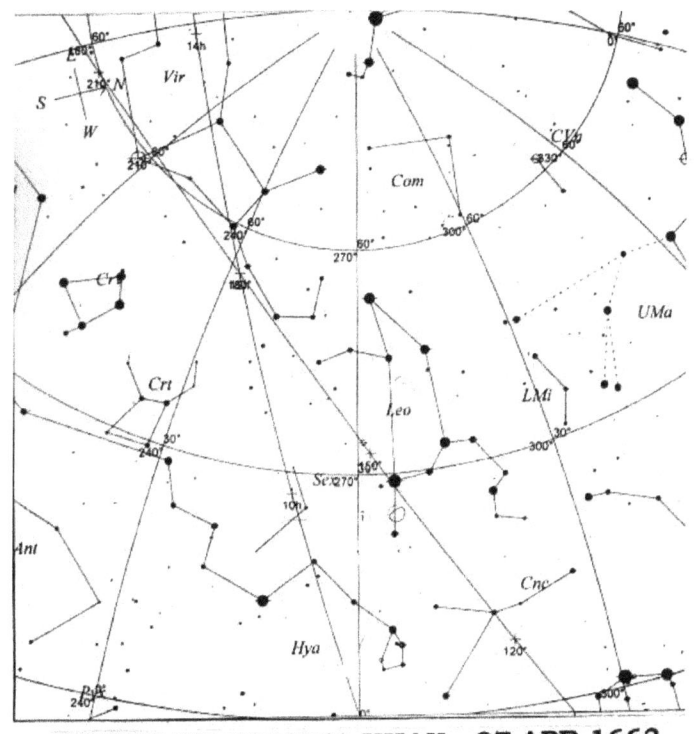

STRIKE ON SHAISTA KHAN - 07 APR 1663

Fig 8/4

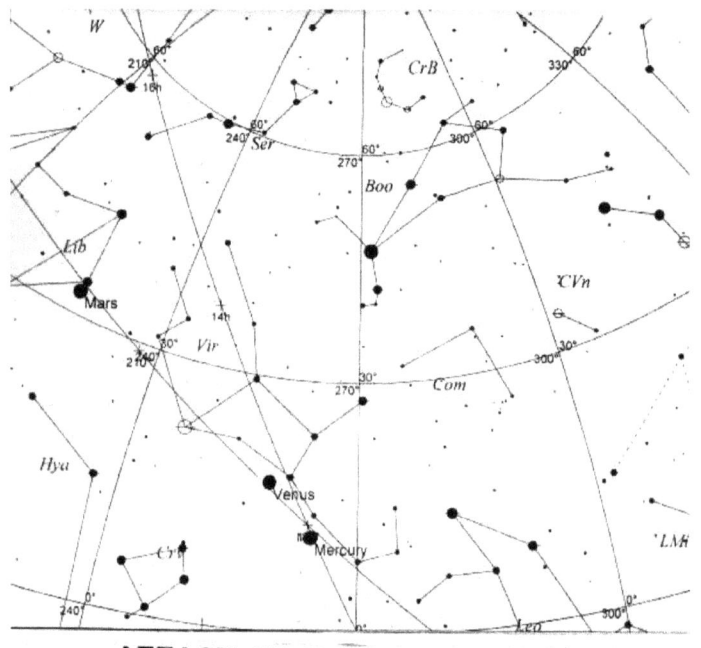

ATTACK ON SURAT - 06 JAN 1664

Fig 8/5

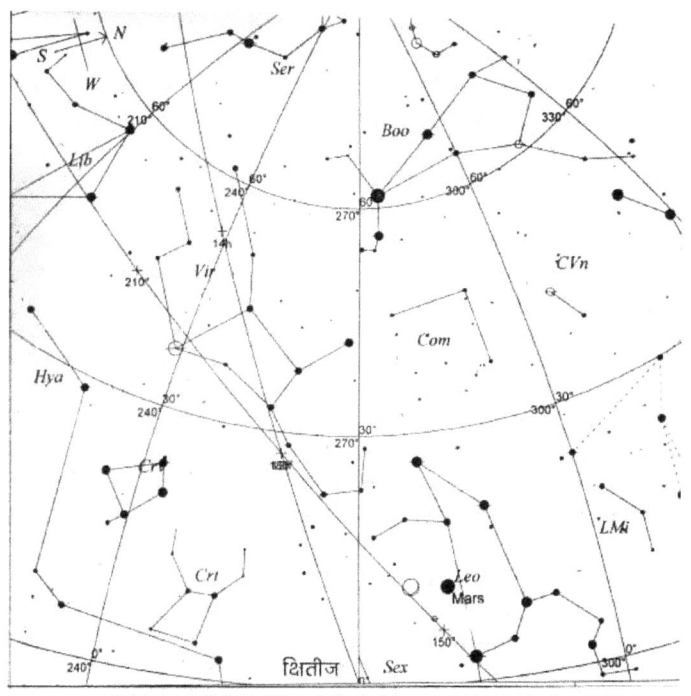

ESCAPE FROM AGRA - 17 AUG 1666

Fig 8 / 6

Legacy of Shivaji Raje

1680 to 1707

We know of the efforts made by Aurangzeb to convert the Hindu population to Islam from 1679 by the application of Jizya. Then in 1682 he attacked Deccan with an army of 500,000 and went all the way south to Jinji near Chennai. In this 25 year war we saw that in the beginning Aurangzeb had the upper hand but bit by bit the Marathas clawed back. They beat him back and he started retreating. But ultimately, he died a frustrated man and was buried in Khuldabad, near Aurangabad.

After Aurangzeb's death (1707 to 1759)

The Maratha Empire became a major power in the Indian subcontinent after the demise of Aurangzeb in 1707. The following three maps show the rise and fall of the Mughals

1-Akbar1605

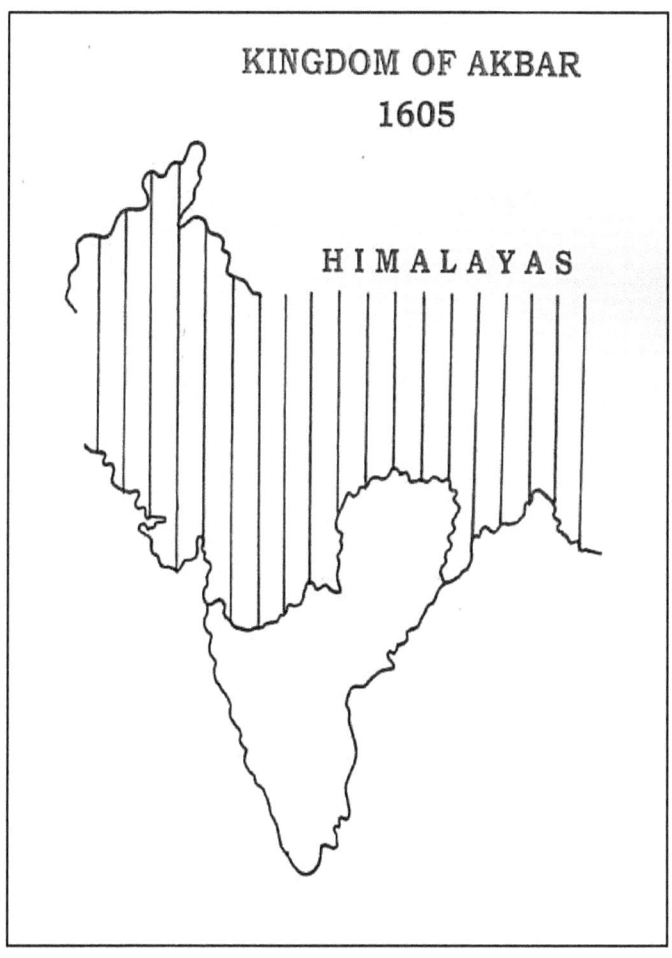

Map 8/ 7

2. Aurangzeb 1707

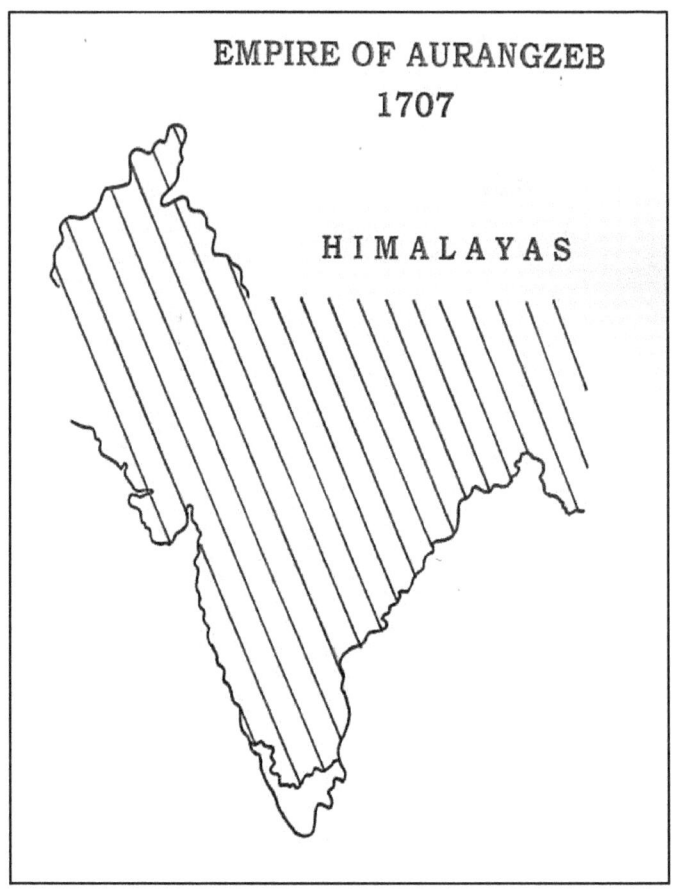

Map 8/ 8

3. Bajirao 1759.

**INDIA
HIGH TIDE OF THE MARATHA EMPIRE
JULY 1759**

52 YEARS AFTER DEATH OF AURANGZEB

Map 8/ 9

In 1759, Bajirao Peshwa had extended the Maratha Empire from Jinji in the South to Attock in the North i.e. present-day Peshawar.

CHAPTER NINE

Epilogue

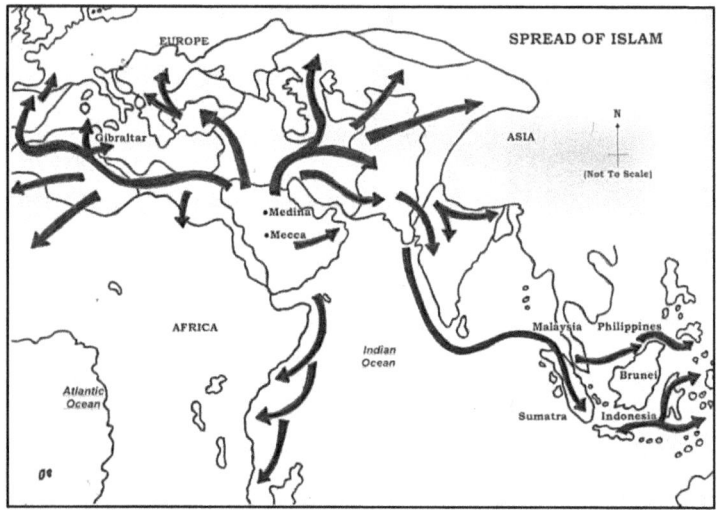

Map 9/1

The above map 9/1 shows the Muslim conquest of the world.

It shows that Mecca and Medina were conquered during the prophet's life time.

The Official religion today is Sunni Islam.

Egypt, Basra, Bagdad, Jerusalem, Persia, Turkestan, Iraq, Afghanistan, Oman, Saudi Arabia, Yemen and Iran were conquered in the seventh century. Their official religion is Sunni Islam. Iran is Shia.

Libia, Sudan, Mali, Niger, Ethiopia in North Africa were conquered by 800 to 1200 AD.

Their official religion is Sunni Islam.

Brunei: Malaysia and Indonesia were captured from 1300 to 1500 AD. Islam is the one of the official religions.

In India, Islam came in about 1000 AD. First, they were plunderers but later by the time of Akbar they had decided to settle down and became rulers.

The sultanates that ruled India after 1000 AD are enumerated below:

Qutub-ud-din Aibak and Altmash (1206- 1235 AD)

Razia Begum (1236 -1239 AD)

Ghias-ud-din Balban (1266- 1286 AD)

Khilji Dynasty (1290 -1320 AD)

The Tughlaq Dynasty (1320- 1414 AD)

Firoz Shah Tughlaq (1351 -1388 AD)

The Saiyad- Lodi Dynasties (1451- 1526 AD)

The Bahmani Kingdom (1347 -1526 AD)

The Empire of Vijayanagar (1336- 1565 AD)

The Mughal Dynasty

Zahir-ud-din Babur (1526- 1530 AD)

Nasir-ud-din Humayun (1530- 1540 AD)

Sher Shah Suri (1540 -1555 AD)

Akbar the Great (1556- 1605 AD)

Jahangir and Nurjahan (1605- 1627 AD)

Shah Jahan (1627- 1658 AD)

Aurangzeb Alamgir (1658 -1707 AD)

Aurangzeb died in 1707.

Long before the death of Aurangzeb, the Marathas began an expansion northward. They crossed the Narmada, the traditional boundary between the northern plains and the southern peninsula. By 1758, hardly fifty years after Aurangzeb's death, the Marathas had conquered Delhi and the empire extended from Cuttack to Attock near Peshawar. What six Mughal emperors conquered in 1504- 1707 (almost 200 years); the Marathas took back in hardly fifty years.

By 1759, Bajirao Peshwa had extended the Maratha Empire till Attock in present day Peshawar. The grand Mughal Empire ceased to exist. In fact, when Abdali attacked Delhi it was the Marathas who went from Pune to fight for the Mughals at Panipat.

This has never happened in the history of Islam. Once conquered that land through forced conversion and Jizya turned from Dar ul Harab to Dar ul Islam.

As seen in Map 9/ 2 the mighty bigot Aurangzeb with his huge army and immense treasure could not subjugate the Hindus.

India is still largely Hindu and the cause is Shivaji Raje.

As Kavi Bhushan put it *"Temples fell, everywhere the flag of Ali fluttered, the Raoranes (braves) of the land ran away, hid themselves here and there, Devi Parvati and Lord Ganesh could not show their chamatkar, they also hid themselves, Pir and Paigambar took the place (awtar), the punyayi (good deeds) of the sadhus and sants was wasted and the effect of Rab increased. The arts of Kashi were destroyed, Mathura became a masjid. In such circumstances if Shivaji Raje was not born, everyone would be circumcised."*

CHAPTER TEN

Afzal Khan's Tomb Today

Seen in the Fig 10/1 is the Afzal Khan's tomb on Pratapgad in 1916.
Source: Mahabaleshwar by D.B. Parasnis

Fig 10/ 1

Until over two decades ago, the grave of Afzal Khan was lying unnoticed in a jerkwater condition. One could see it on the right side after climbing a few steps after passing the main entrance gate of the fort. However, it gained prominence only after some Muslim ascetics in the 2000s claimed the grave and decided to build a shelter over it. According to unverified shreds of information, the state forest department had allotted reserved land to the dargah trust and allowed new construction in the tomb's vicinity a decade ago.

Gradually over a decade, a permanent structure with an arcade from all the four sides was raised on the grave. Covered with a tapering roof of asbestos sheets, the interior is said to have independent rooms for wandering Muslim ascetics who often take refuge in the newly developed 'Shrine'.

Fig10/2

Soon, Afzal Khan – the tyrant from Bijapur who was a staunch enemy of Shivaji Raje, was being gloried in Shivaji Maharaj's own fort.

Apparently, the construction was carried out illegally in the name of a "Hazrat Mohammed Afzal Khan Memorial Trust" which had occupied around 5,500 square feet space on the fort. Soon an Urs started being celebrated.

Shri Milind Ekbote   Smt Vijaya Bhosle

It was in 1996 that Shri Milind Ekbote started an Andolan against the illegal constructions of that Afzal tomb. A detailed discussion is beyond the scope of this book. We shall briefly touch upon it.

By 2001 the andolan had grown and luminaries like Shri Sambhaji Bhide supported it.

In 2002 after a andolan at Azad Maidan headed by Shri Ekbote, the then home minister Shri R R Patil stopped the Urs.

In 2003 Shri Ekbote roped in the Vishwa Hindu Parishad but they were also not to go beyond Pachwad (near Wai). Smt Vijaya Bhosle who was apart of the andolan laid down on the road in protest.

The Pratapgad Utsav Samiti, headed by local corporator Milind Ekbote and backed by Vijayatai Bhonsale had filed public interest litigation in 2007 to remove the dargah at the tomb of Afzal Khan who was killed by Chhatrapati Shivaji Raje at Pratapgad. On 12 October 2008, a bench of Justice J N Patel and Justice S K Kathawala of Bombay High Court had ordered to demolish the illegal structure. The order stated that the land belonged to the forest department and hence no structure would be allowed there.

The bench comprising Justices D K Jain and Anil Dave in its order on February 13, 2012, said the SPL filed by the state government will be dismissed if the government fails to file a better affidavit.

In 2017, PIL was again submitted to the Bombay High Court after which a Bench comprising of Justices S C Dharmadhikari and B P Colabawalla in its ruling gave an ultimatum to the government to bring down the structure.

It may be added here that Adv. Nitin Pradhan appeared for in the case pro bono ie he did not charge any fees.

In 2024 The Chief Minister has constituted the Pratapgad Development Authority of which Shri Milind Ekbote has been appointed as a Committee Member.

During this whole process Shri Milind Ekbote was jailed seventeen times.

IN THE HIGH COURT OF JUDICATURE AT BOMBAY
CIVIL APPELLATE JURISDICTION
PUBLIC INTEREST LITIGATION NO.141 OF 2007

Milind Ramakant Ekbote ..Petitioner
Vs.
The State of Maharashtra & Ors. ..Respondents

Ms.Shubhada Khot for the petitioner
Ms.J.S.Pawar, Addl.G.P. for respondent nos.1

**CORAM : J.N.PATEL &
S.J.KATHAWALA, JJ.**
DATED : 15TH OCTOBER, 2008

P.C.:

1. In view of the fact that this court has already disposed of Writ Petition No.142 of 2004 by judgment and order dated 30.01.2008 which has also disposed of other connected matters i.e. Criminal Writ Petition No.1966 of 2004 and Criminal Writ Petition No.1862 of 2004, it is not necessary for us to further entertain the Writ Petition which is based on subsequent development on the subject land relating to unauthorised construction.

2. It is submitted by the learned counsel for the petitioner that the proposal to regularise unauthorised construction is forwarded to the State Government so as to avoid implementation of the orders of this court.

3. The learned Addl.G.P. points out to this court that the issue has been dealt by the bench which has disposed of Writ Petition No.142 of 2004. We are quite sure that the State would refrain from regularising any construction on the subject land for two reasons. Firstly, this court has directed the authorities to remove encroachment and unauthorised construction and secondly, the land in question is forest land and under the Forest (Conservation) Act, forest land cannot be used for non forest purpose unless permission of specially constituted committee under the Ministry of Environment and Forest is obtained as held by the Supreme Court in the case of **T.N.Godavarman Thirumulpad vs. Union of India and Ors. reported in 2008 (6) Scale 499.**

4. Petition is disposed of.

5. After we dictated the order, the learned Addl G.P. states that she may be granted time to file affidavit in reply in the matter. In our view, as the State has failed to file any affidavit in reply though the petition is pending since long and an identical petition has been disposed of after considering the affidavit in reply filed by the State in Public Interest Litigation No.142 of 2004, we do not think any opportunity should be given to the State in the matter. In case of any contingency, the State can always approach this court and seek appropriate direction / order by moving the court through interim application.

(J.N. PATEL, J)

(S.J. KATHAWALA, J)

IN THE HIGH COURT OF JUDICATURE AT BOMBAY
CIVIL APPELLATE JURISDICTION

CONTEMPT PETITION NO. 267 OF 2010

Mr. Milind Ramakant Ekbote }   Petitioner
versus
The State of Maharashtra }
and Ors. }   Respondents

Ms. Shubadha Khot i/b. Ms. Ameeta Kuttikrishnan for the petitioner.

Ms. Aparna D. Vhatkar – AGP for respondent nos. 1 and 2.

Mr. N. D. Sharma for respondent no. 3.

                               CORAM :- S. C. DHARMADHIKARI & B. P. COLABAWALLA, JJ.

                               DATED :- JANUARY 25, 2017

P.C. :-

1. We are informed by the petitioner's counsel Ms. Khot that despite an order passed by this court in the year 2008 so as to ensure demolition of all unauthorised structures in forest area, particularly at Pratapgad, District Satara, near Mahabaleshwar, the authorities have yet to remove all the unauthorised construction and structures at the site.

2. There are several affidavits, which have been filed in this contempt petition, which also has remained pending for nearly 7

years. Till date, complete compliance of the order passed by this court is not reported, as complained by Ms. Khot.

3. We would like the Government Pleader to take proper instructions and file an affidavit disclosing the details of the demolition activities carried out with number of structures, their location and date of construction and date of demolition. Further, we would like the affidavit to state the names of all the officials, who are in-charge of ensuring that no unauthorised construction comes up in the forest area. If such details are not forthcoming, we would not hesitate to summon the Conservator of Forest and thereafter, he would be personally liable for complete compliance with what this order contemplates and particularly in this PIL. We are of the clear opinion, as complained by Ms. Khot, that the order is not vague or incapable of compliance.

(B.P.COLABAWALLA, J.)   (S.C.DHARMADHIKARI, J.)

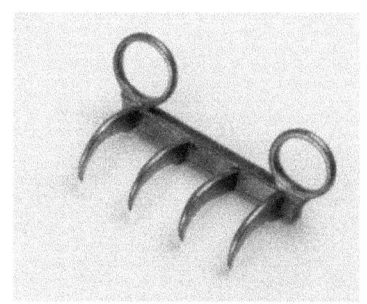 

Wagh Nakh presented to James Grant Duff
Fig 10/3

Details of the Wagh Nakh as entered in the Victoria and Albert Museum

Fig 10/ 4

Shri Vinod Roshan D'souza
Fig 10/5

Letter to Mr Vinod Roshan D'souza from Buckingham Palace.

BUCKINGHAM PALACE

14th October, 2021

Dear Mr D'souza,

I am writing to thank you for your letter to The Queen dated 5th October 2021 in which you request to know how many letters you have sent to Her Majesty and Members of The Royal Family over the last 12 years.

I can tell you that we have a record of 101 letters or messages being received over this period.

Although it is not possible to reply to every letter sent to The Queen or her family, I am to thank you for your support for Her Majesty which is appreciated.

Yours sincerely,

Correspondence Manager

Mr Vinod Roshan D'souza

Fig 10/ 6

Danpatta : State Weapon of Maharashtra

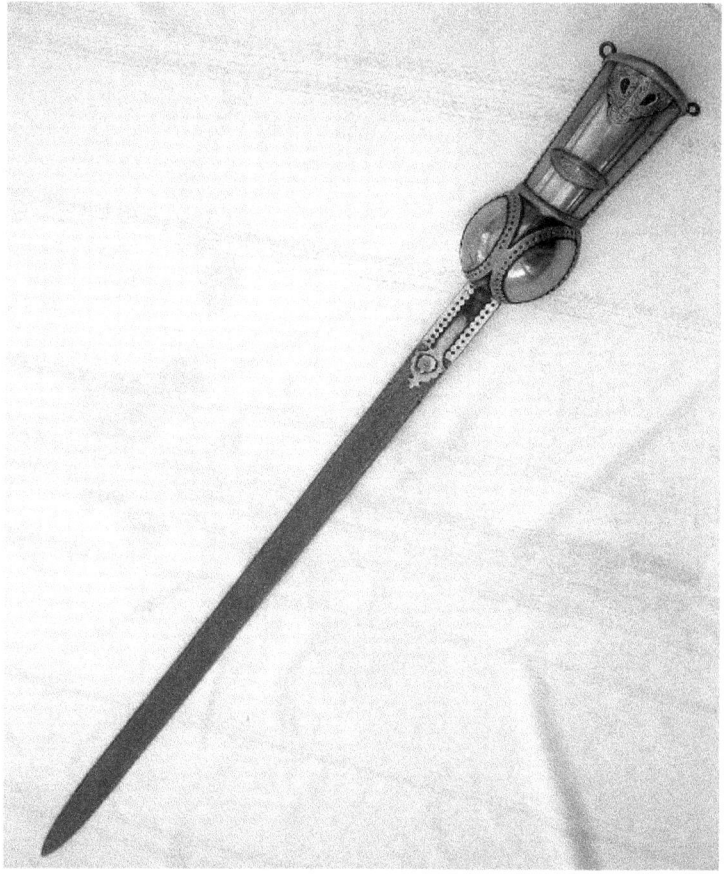

An ornamental pata with a 41" (104 cm) blade

Fig 10 / 7

The *patta or danpatta* is a sword, originating from the Indian subcontinent, with a gauntlet integrated as a handguard. Often referred to in its native Marathi as a *dandpatta*, it is commonly called a gauntlet-sword in English.

The characteristic feature of the pata is its hilt which takes the form of a half-gauntlet, the inside of which is usually padded. The hilt is attached to the blade by decorative arms that extend forward on both sides of the blade.

The hilt also has a long cuff which is usually decorated and embellished with gold and silver. The swordsman holds the weapon by gripping a crossbar inside the gauntlet. The cuff is held close to the forearm by another bar or chain.

The pata is most commonly paired with either a shield or another pata, though it can also be used with a javelin, axe, or belt. The restrictive handle was particularly suited to the stiff-wristed style of South Asian swordsmanship. Despite its shape, the pata is used primarily for cutting rather than thrusting. The extended grip provided by the forearm permits powerful slashes but restricts any thrusts.

Miniature paintings show that the pata was also wielded by mounted cavalry, which has led some modern collectors to erroneously conclude that the weapon was used for thrusting from horseback. However, the restriction on wrist movement would have made it difficult to dislodge the pata from an opponent's body, and doing so while mounted would most likely cause the swordsmen to fall off their horses. Rather, it is more probable that the pata was used in cut-and-run tactics, characteristic of the Maratha army. Cutting technique was practiced by slicing fruit on the ground like lemons or limes without touching the ground. This was and still is a common method of demonstration, often using a flexible blade to facilitate the trick. It is said that Maratha warriors would swing the pata in circular movement like whirlwind when encircled before they fell, so as to maximize the casualties on the opposition. It was to be effective when two soldiers fought together as pairs.

"पट्टा" (दांडपट्टा) या शस्त्रास "राज्य शस्त्र" म्हणून घोषित करण्याबाबत.

महाराष्ट्र शासन
पर्यटन व सांस्कृतिक कार्य विभाग
शासन निर्णय क्रमांक: मुयसं २०२४/प्र.क्र.९८/सां.का.३
हुतात्मा राजगुरू चौक, मादाम कामा मार्ग,
मंत्रालय, मुंबई ४०० ०३२
दिनांक : १९ फेब्रुवारी, २०२४

वाचा : संचालक, पुरातत्व व वस्तुसंग्रहालय संचालनालय, मुंबई यांचे जा.क्र.तंत्र २०२३/राज्य शस्त्र- पट्टा/२३८५, दिनांक १३.०९.२०२३ चे पत्र.

प्रस्तावना:-

महाराष्ट्राचे आराध्य दैवत असलेल्या छत्रपती शिवाजी महाराजांनी निर्माण केलेले स्वराज्य ही एक जगाच्या इतिहासातील अलौकिक घटना आहे. अटक ते बंगाल पसरलेल्या प्रचंड अशा मराठा साम्राज्याचा पाया छत्रपती शिवाजी महाराजांची युद्धनिती- गनिमी कावा, सह्याद्रीची भौगोलिक रचना व त्यातील दुर्गम किल्ले, चपळ घोडदळ व पोलादी शस्त्रांचा प्रभावी वापर यांच्या आधारे रचला होता. मराठा शस्त्रांमध्ये ढाल-तलवार, पट्टा, भाला, कट्यार, वाघनखे, धनुष्यबाण, ठासणीच्या बंदुका व तोफा यांचा समावेश होतो.

या शस्त्रांमध्ये **"पट्टा"** ज्याला सर्वसाधारण भाषेत दांडपट्टा असे संबोधले जाते, हे एक वैशिष्ट्यपूर्ण शस्त्र आहे. सरळ लांब दुधारी पाते व त्यास पकडण्यासाठी असलेला खोळबा म्हणजे संपूर्ण कोपरापर्यंतचा हात पूर्णपणे धातूच्या आच्छादनाने झाकला जाईल, अशी मूठ असणारे शस्त्र म्हणजे **"पट्टा"** होय. प्राचीन संस्कृत साहित्यात याचा उल्लेख "*पट्टीश*" असा असून संत ज्ञानेश्वरांनी पट्टा या शस्त्राचा उल्लेख "*खड्गलतिका*" म्हणजेच वेलीप्रमाणे लवचिक पाते असलेली तलवार असा केलेला आहे. छत्रपती शिवाजी महाराजांचा उल्लेख असणाऱ्या शिवभारत, समासद बखर व राज्यव्यवहार कोष, अनेक बखरी व ऐतिहासिक साहित्यात "पट्टा" या शस्त्राचा उल्लेख आढळतो. सभासद बखरीमध्ये पट्ट्याचा कुशल वापर करणाऱ्यास "*पटाईत*" असे संबोधलेले आहे. समकालीन पोवाड्यांमध्ये तसेच समकालीन साहित्यातील अनेक घटनांमध्ये मराठा सरदार व मावळ्यांनी **"पट्टा"** हे शस्त्र वापरल्याचे दिसून येते. छत्रपती शिवाजी महाराज व छत्रपती संभाजी महाराज यांच्या काढलेल्या ऐतिहासिक चित्रांमध्ये त्यांनी **"पट्टा"** हे शस्त्र हाती घेतलेले दाखविण्यात आले आहे. अनेक आंतरराष्ट्रीय संशोधकांनी "पट्टा" हे मराठ्यांचे आवडते शस्त्र असल्याचे नमूद केले आहे, तसेच राजस्थानातील अलबार येथील संग्रहालयात पट्ट्याची माहिती मराठ्यांचे प्रमुख शस्त्र म्हणून दिलेली आहे. महाराष्ट्रात पट्ट्याचा वापर साहसी खेळांमध्येही होत असून युद्धांबरोबरच समारंभाच्या आणि सणांच्या प्रसंगी दांडपट्ट्याची साहसी प्रदर्शने होत असत. आजही महाराष्ट्रात मर्दानी खेळ या युद्धकला आखाड्यांमध्ये पट्टा हाताळणे शिकवले जाते. अर्थात "पट्टा" चालवणे ही महाराष्ट्राची आजही जिवंत असणारी लोकसंस्कृती आहे. छत्रपती शिवाजी महाराज व छत्रपती संभाजी महाराज अशा अलौकिक प्रतिभासंपन्न महापुरुषांच्या आणि मावळ्यांच्या जीवनातील **"पट्टा"** हे शस्त्र

Fig 10/8

शासन निर्णय क्रमांकः पुवसं २०२४/प्र.क्र.१८/सां.का.३

महाराष्ट्राच्या चिरंतन स्मृतीत राहावे, यासाठी **"पट्टा"** (सर्वसाधारण भाषेत दांडपट्टा) या शस्त्रास महाराष्ट्राचे राज्य शस्त्र म्हणून घोषित करण्याची बाब शासनाच्या विचाराधीन होती.

शासन निर्णय :-

छत्रपती शिवाजी महाराज यांचा ३५० वा शिवराज्याभिषेक सोहळा व शिवजयंतीचे औचित्य साधून छत्रपती शिवाजी महाराज, छत्रपती संभाजी महाराज तसेच त्यांच्या मावळ्यांनी लढायांमध्ये वापरलेला **"पट्टा"** (सर्वसाधारण भाषेत दांडपट्टा) हा महाराष्ट्राच्या चिरंतन स्मृतीत रहावा, यासाठी **"पट्टा"** (दांडपट्टा) या शस्त्रास महाराष्ट्राचे **"राज्य शस्त्र"** म्हणून या शासन निर्णयाद्वारे घोषित करण्यात येत आहे.

०२. सदर शासन निर्णय महाराष्ट्र शासनाच्या www.maharashtra.gov.in या संकेतस्थळावर उपलब्ध असून त्याचा संकेतांक क्रमांक २०२४०२१९१०३६१६८१२३ असा आहे. हा आदेश डिजीटल स्वाक्षरीने साक्षांकित करुन निर्गमित करण्यात येत आहे.

महाराष्ट्राचे राज्यपाल यांच्या आदेशानुसार व नावाने,

NANDA MARUTI RAUT

(नंदा राऊत)
उप सचिव, महाराष्ट्र शासन

प्रति,

मा. राज्यपाल यांचे प्रधान सचिव, राजभवन, मुंबई.
मा.मुख्यमंत्री यांचे प्रधान सचिव, मंत्रालय, मुंबई.
मा. उप मुख्यमंत्री (गृह), यांचे , खाजगी सचिव, मंत्रालय, मुंबई.
मा. उप मुख्यमंत्री (वित्त व नियोजन), यांचे , खाजगी सचिव, मंत्रालय, मुंबई.
मा. विधानपरिषद सभापती, यांचे खाजगी सचिव, महाराष्ट्र विधिमंडळ, मुंबई.
मा. विधानसभा अध्यक्ष, यांचे खाजगी सचिव, महाराष्ट्र विधिमंडळ, मुंबई.
मा. विरोधीपक्ष नेता, विधानसभा/ विधानपरिषद यांचे खाजगी सचिव.
सर्व मा. मंत्री यांचे खाजगी सचिव, मंत्रालय, मुंबई.
सर्व सन्माननीय विधानमंडळ सदस्य.
मा. मुख्य सचिव, महाराष्ट्र राज्य, मंत्रालय, मुंबई.
सचिव, संस्कृति मंत्रालय, भारत सरकार, नवी दिल्ली
सर्व अप्पर मुख्य सचिव/ प्रधान सचिव/सचिव, मंत्रालय, मुंबई.
महासंचालक, भारतीय पुरातत्व सर्वेक्षण, नवी दिल्ली.
सर्व विभागीय आयुक्त, महाराष्ट्र राज्य.
महासंचालक, माहिती व जनसंपर्क संचालनालय, मंत्रालय, मुंबई
सर्व पोलीस आयुक्त, पोलीस आयुक्तालय कार्यालये, महाराष्ट्र.
आयुक्त, शालेय शिक्षण, महाराष्ट्र राज्य, पुणे
सर्व जिल्हाधिकारी, महाराष्ट्र राज्य.
सर्व जिल्हा पोलीस अधिक्षक, महाराष्ट्र राज्य.

पृष्ठ ३ पैकी २

Fig 10 /8a

शासन निर्णय क्रमांका **पुवर्स २०२४/प्र.क्र.९८/सां.का.३**

सर्व मुख्य कार्यकारी अधिकारी, जिल्हा परिषद, महाराष्ट्र राज्य.
सर्व आयुक्त महानगरपालिका, महाराष्ट्र राज्य.
सर्व उप सचिव/अवर सचिव/ कक्ष अधिकारी, पर्यटन व सांस्कृतिक कार्य विभाग, मंत्रालय, मुंबई.
सर्व मुख्याधिकारी, नगरपंचायत/नगर परिषद, महाराष्ट्र राज्य.
संचालक, पुरातत्व व वस्तुसंग्रहालय संचालनालय, महाराष्ट्र राज्य, मुंबई
संचालक, सांस्कृतिक कार्य संचालनालय, मुंबई
निवड नस्ती, सां.का.३.

Fig 10 /8b

Fig 10/9

Shri Kiran Shinde and Shri Nilesh Sakat along with Shri Sudhir Mungatiwar, Minister of Cultural Affairs, Maharashtra State, who were instrumental in the Dandpatta being declared as the Weapon of Maharashtra.

(GR/patta/ 2385 dt 19/ 02 /2023)

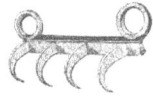

Appendix

Adnyandas cha Powada (Ballad)

Shivaji's victory over Afzal Khan caught the popular imagination of the local public, and ballads glorifying the event were sung by wandering bards (gondhalis). The victory is also glorified in the local literature (Powada). It has four lines with a rhyme on the second and fourth line. It is a simple song, usually slow and sentimental.

The Afzal Khan Vadh equates Shivaji to Rama, and Afzal Khan to Ravana. The Shiva-Bharata similarly describes Shivaji as an avatar of Vishnu, while portraying Afzal Khan as a demonic incarnation. The Shri-Shiva-Prabhuche compares the conflict to the legendary Kurukshetra War, equating Shivaji to Bhima and Afzal Khan to Duryodhana.

"The powada (Marathi: पोवाडा) is a genre of Marathi poetry that was during the late 17th century in India. Powada, which means 'to glorify', is a traditional Marathi ballad that traces its history to more than 750 years. Powadas often glorified and celebrated deeds of popular folk figures and leaders such as Chhatrapati Shivaji and Tanaji Malusare, and were also written to raise awareness on social issues such as female foeticide, dowry and corruption. Powadas were also used as a medium to create awareness during Samyukta Maharashtra movement.

Powada is also a genre of poetry popular in Uttarakhand, specifically that glorifies warriors. It is popular in Kumaun and Garhwal regions of the state and is sung, performed, or narrated on various occasions. It is also known as "Bhada".

During the Maratha Confederacy rule, several celebrated Shahir poet-singers, which include Ram Joshi (1762–1812), Anant Phandi (1744–1819), Honaji Bala (1754–1844) and Prabhakar (1769–

1843), Annabhau Sathe (1920 - 1969), Atmaram Patil and Amar Sheikh composed a number of powadas.

About sixty powadas were collected by Harry Arbuthnot Acworth and S. T. Shaligram and published under the title, The Saga of Historical Heroic Men and Women (**इतिहास प्रसिद्ध महापुरुषांचे व स्त्रियांचे पोवाडे**) in 1891. Out of these, ten powadas were translated into English verse by H. A. Acworth and published as Ballads of the Marathas in 1894."

चौक १

माझें नमन आधी गणा । सकळिक ऐका चित्त देऊन ॥
नमियेली सारज्या । ल्याली जडिताचें भूषण ॥
अज्ञानदासाचें वचन । नमिला सद्गुरु नारायण ॥
सद् गुरुच्या प्रसादें । संपूर्ण अंबेचें वरदान ॥
गाइन वजिराचें भांडण । भोसल्या सरजा दलभंजन ॥
फौजेवर लोटतां । यशवंत खंडेश्वरी प्रसन्न ॥
अज्ञानदास बोले वचन । गाइन राजाचें भांडण ॥
देश इलाइत । काबिज केलें तळकोंकण ॥१॥

Verse 1- The bard (poet singer) Adyandas first bows down to Ganapati, Lord Vishnu and Saraswati Devi. The Shahir (bard) says he is going to describe the defeat of the Bijapuri army sent to attack the throne of the Bhosle family. This attack is because Shivaji Raje has captured many (Adilshahi) lands especially the Konkan.

चौक २

गड मी राजाचे गाईन । कोहज माहुली भर्जन ॥
पारगड कर्नाळा । प्रबलगड आहे संगिन ॥
मस्त तळा आणि घोसाळा । रोहरी आनसवाडी दोन ॥
कारला कासागड मंडन । दर्यांत दिसताती दोन ॥
गड बिरवाडी पांचकोन । सुरगड अवचितगड भूषण ॥

कुबल गड भीरिका कुर्डुगडाचें चांगुलपण ॥
धोडप तळकोंकणचे किल्ले, घाटावरले गड गाइन ॥२॥

Verse 2 - Here he describes the forts captured by Shivaji Raje namely Kohaz, Mahuli, Pargad, Karnala, Tale, Ghosale, Rohri, Anaswadi, Kasgad, Mandangad, Awchitgad, Kubalgad and Ghodap.

चौक ३

गड आहे रोहिडा । जामली प्रतापगड मंडन ॥
मकरंदगड वांसोट । सिंहगड वृंदावन ॥
पुरंधराचें चांगुलपण । उंची झुलवा देत गगन ॥
सोन्याची सुवेळा आहे राजगड संगिन ॥
कोंडाण्यापासून तोरणा वर्ता । कोर रेखिली घाटमाथा ॥
तुंग आणि तुकोना । विसापुर लोहगड झुलता ॥
गड राहेरीची अवस्था । तीन पायऱ्या सोन्याच्या तक्ता ॥
दुसरा प्रतापगड पाहतां । अवघड दिसे घाटमाथा ॥३॥

Verse 3 - Here he continues with names of forts namely Rohida, Pratapgad of Jawli, Makarandgad, Vasota, Sinhagad, Purandar, Rajgad with the Savela machi, Torna, Tikona, Tung, Visapur, Lohgad, Rairi (Raigad).

चौक ४

मस्त हुडे दुर्गाचे खण । माहाल राजाचे गाइन ॥
पुणे भिस्तका दरगा । शेकसल्ला पीर, पाटण ॥
शिरवळ सुपे देस । घेतला ज्यानें इंदापुरा पासुन ॥
महाड गोरेगांवापासून । घेतले शिणगारपूर पाटण ॥
असे तुळजेचे परिपूर्ण । सोडविलें चवदा ताल कोंकण ।
घेतली बारा बंदरें । भाग्य राजाचें संगिन ॥४॥

Verse 4 - After the forts, the bard enumerates the areas that were under Shivaji Raje namely Pune, Shekhsalla i.e. old Pune, Patan, Supe, Indapur, Mahad and from Goregaon to Mahad. Twelve ports and Konkan areas.

चौक ५

देश दुनिया काबिज केली । बारा माउळें घेतलीं ॥
चंद्रराव कैद केला । त्याची गड जाउली घेतली ॥
चेतपाउली काबिज केली । ठाणीं राजाचीं बैसलीं ॥
घेतली जाउली न् माहुली । कल्याण भिवंडी काबिज केली ॥
सोडविलें तळकोंकण । चेउलीं ठाणीं बैसविलीं ॥
कुबल, बांकी घेरें । शिवराजाच्या हाता आलीं ॥
मुलाना हामाद । फिर्याद बाच्छायाप गेली ॥
बाच्छायजादी क्रोधा आली । जैशी अग्न परजळली ॥
जित धरावा राजाला । कुलवजिरांला खबर दिली ॥५॥

Verse 5 - Shivaji Raje took the twelve Mavals, he also imprisoned Chandrarao More and took his Forts and Jawli. In Mahuli, Kalyan, Cheul in place of Bijapur's Adilshahi there were Maratha outposts. All such places which were difficult to capture and had beautiful dwellings were now under the rule of Shivaji Raje. Maulana Hamid complained about all this to Bijapur's Adilshahi. On hearing this news Badshah was very angry and he summoned all his sardars for discussion.

चौक ६

बाच्छाय(ये) पाठविले प्रमाण । वजीर बोलावा तमाम ॥
अबदुलखान, रस्तुम जुमा ॥ सिद्दी हिलाल, मुशेखान ॥
मेळविलें वजिरांला । बाच्छाय बोलावी कवणाला ? ॥
बोलावी बाजी घोरपडयाला । घाटग्या जुंझाररायाला ॥
बोलावी खऱ्या कोबाजीला । त्या नाइकजी पांढऱ्याला ॥

देवकांत्या जीवाजीला । मंबाजी भोसल्याला ॥
बावीस उंबराव मिळुनी । आले बाच्छाय सभेला ॥६॥

Verse 6 - As per the Badshah's angry summons, 22 sardars like Abdulla Khan (Afzal), Rustam e Jama, Siddi Hillal, Muse Khan, Baji Ghorpade, Zunzarrao Ghatge, Kobaji Khare, Naikji Pandhre, Jiwaji Devkatte and Mambaji Bhosle came for the meeting.

चौक ७

बाच्छायजादा पुसे वजीरांला । धरीसा आहे कोण शिवराजाला ॥
बावीस उंबराव आले सभेला । विडा पैजेचा मांडिला ॥
सवाई अबदुल्या बोलला । 'जिता पकडूं मैं राजाला' ।
निरोप दिला कुल्वजिराला । अबदुल सदरे नवाजिला ॥
विडा पैजेचा घेतला (म्हणून) । तुरा मोत्याचा लाविला ॥
गळांअ घातलीं पदकें । खान विजापुरीं बोलला ॥
फिरंग घोडा सदरे दिला । बाच्छायानें नवाजीला ॥
तीवरसांची मोहीम । घेऊन अबदुल्या चालला ॥७॥

Verse 7 - Badshah challenged these main sardars "who among you can imprison Shivaji Raje and bring him here." Afzal Khan said "he would bring Shivaji here alive." An over joyed Adilshahi felicitated Afzal Khan in the darbar. Because Afzal Khan had accepted the challenge, Adilshah presented a hackle of pearls in Afzal Khan's headgear. He was presented with a garland of medals round his neck and an Arabian horse and sent on this mission. He was supplied with enough provisions to last three years.

चौक ८

खान कटकबंद केला । कोटाबाहेर डेरा दिला ॥
मोठा अपशकुन जाहला । फत्यालसकरा हत्ती मेला ॥
खबर गेली बाच्छायाला । बिनीचा हत्ती पाठविला ॥
बारा हजार घोडा । अबदुलखानालागीं दिला ॥८॥

Verse 8 - Khan gathered an army for this expidition just outside Bijapur. Afzal Khan's principal elephant Fateh Lashkar died and this was considered to be a bad omen. In order to boost the morale of Afzal Khan, the Badshah presented him with his own royal elephant.

चौक ९
संगात कुंजर मस्त हत्ती । घेतली झगडयाची मस्तुती ॥
आरोब्याच्या गाडया । कोतवालतेजी धांवा घेती ।
सातशें उंट आहे बाणांचा । करडा लष्करी खानाचा ।
वजीर अबदुलखान । त्याच्या दळाची गणती ।
बारा हजार घोडा । उंबराव ताबिन चालती ॥९॥

Verse 9- The Khan commenced his campaign with many such ferocious elephants. There were numerous carriages full of provisions and gunpowder that were moving fast and the kotwals found it difficult to maintain order. There were 12,000 camels laden with arrows. The strong 12,000 cavalry took off under the strict discipline of Afzal Khan.

चौक १०
तेथुनि कुच केलें कटकाला । अबदुल फौजेनें चालिला ॥
मजलीवर मजल । अबदुल तुळजापुरा आला ॥
फोडिली तुळजा । वरती मसुदच बांधिली ॥
मसुद बांधुनी । पुढें गाय जब केली ॥
अबदुलखान फोडी देवीला । 'कांहीं एक अजमत दाव मला' ॥
कोपली भद्रकाली । बांधुनी शिवराजाप दिला ।
अंबा गेली सपनांत (ला) । कांहीं एक बोल शिवराजाला ॥
'बत्तीस दातांचा बोकड । आला वधायाला' ॥१०॥

Verse 10 - Afzal Khan marched stage by stage to Tuljapur. He mocked the Goddess to show him her power. So saying he broke up the idol of the Goddess and slaughtered a cow in the sanctum sanctorum. He then converted the temple into a mosque.

An enraged Bhadrakali Goddess at that very moment plotted his death by the hands of Shivaji Raje. The Jagadamba Devi appeared in the dreams of Shivaji Raje and ordered that "I am sending you a thirty two toothed goat. Slaughter him"

चौक ११

तेथून कुच केलें कटकाला । अबदुल दरमजली चालिला ॥
मजलीवर मजल । अबदुल माणकेश्वरा आला ॥
तेव्हां त्या अबदुलखानानें । हाल मांडिले देवाला ॥
तेथुनि कुच केलें कटकाला । अबदुल फौजेनें चालिला ॥
मजलीवर मजल । अबदुल करकंभोशा आला ॥
तेथुनि कुच केलें कटकाला । अबदुल दरमजली चालिला ॥
मजलीवर मजल । वेगीं पंढरपुरा आला ॥
फोडिला विठोबा । पुंडलिक पाण्यात टाकिला ॥११॥

Verse 11 - Afzal Khan's army proceeded stage by stage from Tuljapur to Mankeshwar. Here again he shattered the idol of the Goddess and defiled the purity of the temple. He then galloped to Pandharpur where he broke the idol of Vithal and threw the idol of Pundalik in the river.

चौक १२

खान (नें) कुच केलें कटकाला । अबदुल फौजेनें चालिला ॥
मजलीवर मजल । वेगीं महादेवासी आला ॥
तेव्हां त्या अबदुलखानानें । दंड बांधिला शंभुला ॥
हाल हिंदुच्या देवाला । अबदुलखान (नें) धाक लाविला ॥
तेथुनि कुच केलें कटकाला । अबदुल दरमजली चालिला ।
मजलीवर मजल । अबदुल रहिमतपुरा आला ॥१२॥

Verse 12 - Khan was now galloping rapidly towards Mahadev (Shiva) Shikhar Shingnapur. He defiled the temples there and committed such atrocities as though like the demons in ancient times he wanted to terrorize the Gods and Goddesses. Later Khan made his way to Swarajya via Rahimatpur.

चौक १३
अबदुल आलासे बोलती । धाकें गड किल्ले कांपती ॥
वजीर उंबराव बोलती । 'शिवाजीस गडे कोंडू', म्हणती ।
अबदुल सारा आहे किती । त्याच्या दळाची गणती ॥
बारा हजार घोडा । उंबराव ताबिन चालती ॥
सौंदळीं भांडतां । मग कणकीला मीठ किती ? ॥१३॥

Verse 13 - All the forts started trembling due to the terror of Afzal Khan. His sardar's started boasting that they would trap Shivaji Raje in his fort. Compared to Afzal Khan's army Shivaji Raje's Swarajya was like salt in wheat dough.

चौक १४
तेथुनि कुच केलें कटकाला । अबदुल वांईलागी आला ॥
आपुल्या मुलखांत राहिला । कोट बांधुन पिंजरा केला ॥
बरेपणाचा कागद (देउन) । हेजिब महाराजाप गेला ॥
राजा पुण्यात मस्त झाला । देश पाठीशीं घेतला ॥
सोडून दिले किल्ले । डेरा जाऊलींत दिला ॥
राजा जाऊलींत राहिला । हेजिब अबदुल्याचा आला ॥१४॥

Verse 14 - Afzal Khan came from Rahimatpur to Wai. Since previously he was the Subhedar of Wai, he made his camp like a seasoned general. He made his head-quarters at the pre-existing Subhedar Wada (mansion). From his base he sent a letter through his envoy to Shivaji Raje, where in he assured Shivaji Raje that he had no treachery in his mind. At this time Shivaji Raje had moved from the desh i.e. (Rajgad, Pune) to Jawli (Pratapgad, Mahabaleshwar). Khan's envoy came to meet him there.

चौक १५

हेजिब बोले महाराजाला । 'खान बच्यापणाशीं आला ॥
खानाला भेटतां । थोर बाच्छाये सल्ला झाला' ॥
राजा बोले हेजिबाला । 'कशाला बोलवितां वांईला ? ॥
किल्ले गड कोट । दवलत खानाच्या हवाला ॥
जाऊली खानाच्या हवाला । लिहून देतों हेजिबाला ॥
बैसूं दोघेजण । खान बुध सांगेल आम्हांला' ।
लुगडीं दिलीं हेजिबाला । हेजीब 'बेगीं' रवाना झाला' ॥१५॥

Verse 15 - The envoy said to Shivaji Raje that wishes to meet him with love (friendship). So meet Khan and sign a treaty. At this Shivaji Raje said "For such a small matter why call me to Wai? When we meet I shall present all my forts and fortresses to Khan. Not only that, where we are today, I shall present even Jawli to Khan. When we both meet Khan will instruct me as to what benefits me. Thus he felicitated the envoy and presented him with robes of honor. The envoy immediately returned back to Afzal Khan.

चौक १६

हेजिबाची खबर ऐकुनी । अबदुल महाभुजंग झाला ॥
अबदुलखान (नें) कउल दिला । रोटीपीर पाठविला ॥
'भिउ नको शिवाजी भाई । आहे तेरा मेरा सल्ला ॥
तुझे गड तुझ्या हवाला । आणिक दवलत देतों तुला ॥
तुझी थोडीशी गोष्ट । क्रिया शहाजीची आम्हाला' ॥
इकडे कउल पाठविला । (पण) शीलचा राउत निवडिला ॥
हत्तीचे पायीं तोरड । लाविला गजढाळा ।
नदरे पडतां । दस्त करा शिवराजाला ॥१६॥

Verse 16 - When the envoy brought this news of the abject surrender by Shivaji Raje, Afzal Khan started swaying like a cobra in joy and jubilation. To promise that he would not indulge in treachery he sent a piece of bhakri (bajra) with his envoy. The envoy orally delivered the message, "Oh Shivaji Raje, you are like a younger brother to me. We will soon have a treaty, don't be scared of me. Your forts and fortresses will remain with you. I shall present you more territory (from the Badshah) I have promised this to Shahaji Raje." Thus after promising a safe meeting, Shivaji Raje ordered his army to be on the alert. He picked the warriors and the elephants who would accompany him at the meeting. He gave the clarion call that anyone who saw Shivaji Raje should imprison him.

चौक १७

राजा हेजीबासि बोलतो । "खंड काय मला मागतो ॥
चउआगळे चाळीस गड । मी अबदुलखानालागीं देतों ।
मजवर कृपा आहे खानाची । जावर्लीत सदरा सवारितो ॥
तेथें यावें भेटायाला । मी खानाची वाट पाहतों "॥
हेजिब तेथुनि निघाला । अबदुलखानाजवळ आला ॥
अबदुलखानामोहरें । हेजिब (बें) टाकिला प्रमाण ॥
अबदुल पाहतो वाचुन । "खुंटले गनिमाचें मरण" ॥
हाती आले गड किल्ले । खुशी जहाला अबदुलखान ॥१७॥

Verse 17- Shivaji Raje said to Afzal Khan's envoy "how can I pay a tribute to Afzal Khan when I am giving him all my kingdom and all my forty forts. I am building a grand meeting place for Afzal Khan, so he should favor me by visiting me. I await his arrival."

The envoy returned back to Afzal Khan and gave him Shivaji Raje's letter. On reading this letter Afzal Khan's happiness knew no bounds. He felt that the enemy has himself walked into his clutches.

चौक १८

हिगडे सल्ला कउल दिला । खासा राउत निवडिला ॥
चार हजार घोडा । हालका धराया चालला ॥

हर्तींचे पायिं तोरड ज्याला । वरी सोडिल्या गजढाला ॥
फौजामागें फौजा । भार कडक्यानें चालला ॥
रडतोंडीच्या घाटाखालीं । अबदुल सारा उतरुं दिला ॥
इसारत सरज्याच्या लोकांला । ज्यांणीं घाट बळकाविला ॥
मागल्याची खबर नाहीं पुढिल्याला । कटकाची खबर, कैंची त्याला ॥
जाऊं जाणें येऊं नेणें । ही गत झाली अबदुल्याला ॥
जावलींत उतरुनि । अबदुल दिशीभुला जाहला ॥१८॥

Verse 18 - Here Afzal Khan had given a promise of safety but on the other hand he started preparing for war. He took with him an armored cavalry of 4000, the haudas on the elephants were mounted, and the flag was hoisted. Afzal Khan with this huge army descended the Radtondi ghat and marched (towards Pratapgad). The Marathas allowed Afzal Khan's army to (unhindered) come down the mountain pass and go forward. The moment he had done so they took control of the mountain top and thus closed the exit route of Afzal Khan. The pass was narrow, so those behind could not realize the difficulties of those in front, so how could Afzal Khan understand the hardship of the whole army. In this way the Marathas totally deceived the Khan.

चौक १९

राजानी सदरा सवारिल्या । गाद्या पडगाद्या घातल्या ॥
तिवाशा जमखान टाकिले । सदर पिकदाण्या ठेविल्या ॥
सुरंग चारी खांब सदरेचे । वरी घोंस मोतीयांचें ॥
माणिकाच्या भरणी । हारी मोत्यांच्या बसविल्या ॥
दुसरे सदरेची मांडणी । सूर्य लखलखितो गगनीं ।
मणिकाचे ढाळ । सदरे सुवर्णिचें पाणी ॥
काचबंदी पटांगणाचा ढाळ । कापुर कस्तुरी परिमळ ॥१९॥

चौक २०
तिसरे सदरेची मांडणी । हिरे जोडिले खणोखणीं ॥
खासियाचे पलंग । ते ठेवोनी मध्यस्थानीं ॥
वाळियाच्या झांजी । दबण्याचे कुंड घालोनी ॥
बराणपुरी चिटाचे । आडोआड पडदे बांधुनी ॥
चाहुंकोनी चारी समया । चांदवा जडिताचा बांधोनी ॥
घोंस मोतियांचे । वर ठिकडी नानापरिची ॥
अवघी जडिताची लावणी । हिरे जोडिले खणोखणीं ॥
बहुत सवारिल्या सदरा ॥ ऐशी नाहीं देखिल्या कोणी ॥२०॥

Verse 19/20 Here the king (Shivaji) started to build Sadar- a place for meeting the Khan. They used fine mattresses, laid heavy carpets, and placed golden spittoons on the tripods. The pillar of the tent was decorated with a necklace of pearls, diamonds, and rubies. The aroma of camphor musk perfumed the whole area.

Diamonds were added at various places (in the canopy) and the comfortable seats were placed in the middle of the tent where these two personalities were meeting. Curtains made from Khus were added (for cooling the place), and Davana (Artemisia pallens) were added to the water in small pools (for aroma). The main meeting place was segregated with the use of Burhanpuri cloth. Fourr big brass lamps (Samai) were kept at four corners (to illuminate the place) which created a scene as if moonlight was spread all around. He (Afzal Khan) said that he had seen many Sadras (visiting places) but no one had ever seen such a lavishly decorated meeting place.

चौक २१
राजानीं सदरा सवारिल्या । हेजिब अबदुल्यास धाडिला ॥
मोरो ब्राह्मण पाठविला । अबदुलखानासी बोलाविला ॥
"चार हजार घोडा । कोण्या कामास्तव आणिला ?" (म्हणून) त्यानें बाहेर निराळा ठेविला ।

दहा पांचांनिशिं चालिला ॥ "एकांतीच्या गोष्टी ।
तेथें दहा पांच कशाला ॥ पालखी दुर करा भोईयाला ।"
खासा अबदुल चालला ॥ "हात चालावा व्हा । दुर करा" म्हणे खानाला ॥
वस्त्रें केली हेजीबाला । शामराज नवाजीला ॥२१॥

Verse 21- As soon as the meeting place was ready, Shivaji Raje sent the Brahmin Moropant to Afzal Khan. Immediately on seeing that Afzal Khan had started with an army (Moropant) asked why take 4000 horsemen when the meeting is only between the two of you? So saying he convinced Afzal Khan to keep that army at the base. When Afzal Khan came to the meeting place he (Moropant) cleverly said you are going to have a (personal) conversation, so keep away the ten bodyguards and palanquin bearers. Afzal Khan himself stepped forward to the meeting. He gave robes of honor to Moropant and Shamrajpant. (Actually both of them were not present. It was Pantajikaka Gopinath who was present.)

चौक २२

भवानीशंकर प्रसन्न ज्याला । तुळजा मदत शिवराजाला ॥
भोग पुरला खानाचा । अबदुल जावळींत आला ॥
बिनहत्याराविण मोकळा । अबदुल सदरेलागीं आला ।
अबदुल पहिले सदरे गेला । सदर देखुनी सुखी झाला ॥
'ऐशी सदर नव्हती । आमच्या आली इदलशाला ॥"
खान दुसरे सदरे गेला । सदर देखुनि सुखी झाला ॥
'ऐशी सदर नव्हती । नवरंगशा बाच्छायाला" ॥
अबदुल तिसरे सदरे गेला । सदर देखुनि सुखी झाला ॥
"ऐसी सदर नाहीं अवरंगशा बाच्छायाला" ॥ अबदुलखान बोलिला ।
"शिवाजीस आणा भेटायाला" ॥२२॥

Verse 22-Lord Shankar was pleased with Shivaji Raje and the Goddess Tulja bhawani was his benefactor. When he entered

Jawli, Afzal Khan sins were innumerable. Afzal Khan came to the meeting place (shamiana) without any weapons.

When he came to the first (part) of the shamiana he said "even the Adilshah does not have such a shamiana." When he came to the second (part) of the shamiana he said "even the Navrangshah i.e. Shah Jahan does not have such a shamiana." When he came to the third (part) of the shamiana he said "even Aurangzeb does not have such a shamiana."

Now call Shivaji Raje to meet me, said the eager Afzal Khan.

चौक २३

राजा नवगर्जीत बैसला । मोरो, शाम बोलविला ॥
रघुनाथ पेशवे । नारो शंकर पाचारिला ॥
दहातोंडया माणकोजीला । त्या इंगळ्या सुभानजीला ॥
देवकांत्या जीवाजीला । राजानें बोलाविले तुम्हांला ॥
करनखऱ्या सुभानजीला । बेलदारा पिलाजीला ॥
त्या बोबडया बहिरजीला । सरदार आले भेटायाला ॥२३॥

Verse 23- On the fort Shivaji Raje called a war council of his advisors namrly Moropant, Shamrjpant, Raghunath Peshwe, Naro Shankar, Mankoji Dahatonde, Subhanji Ingle, Jiwaji Devkate, Pillaji and Bahirji.

चौक २४

राजा विचारी भल्या लोकांला । "कैसें जावें भेटायाला" ॥
बंककर कृष्णाजी बोलला । "शिवबा सील करा अंगाला" ॥
भगवंताची सील ज्याला---- । आंतून, (तो) बारिक झगा ल्याला ॥
मुसेजरीच्या सुरवारा । सरजा (जें) बंद सोडुन दिला ॥
डावे हातीं बिचवा त्याला (ल्याला) । वाघनख सरज्याच्या पंजाला ।
पटा जिव म्हाल्याप दिला । सरजा बंद सोडुन चालिला ॥२४॥

Verse 24 - Shivaji Raje asked these intelligent people, "what precautions (should I) take while meeting Afzal Khan ?". Krishnaji Bankar suggested "Shivba, wear an armor." Shivaji Raje accepted this advice and wore a finely woven armor. (On top of this) he the wore a dress of interlaced gold, in his left sleeve he inserted a bichwa (double edged curved dagger) and in the left hand he wore tiger claws. He gave his patta (long sword) to Jiwa Mahala. Thus breaking all bonds, the lion went to the meeting.

चौक २५

"माझा रामराम दादानु" ॥ गडच्या गडकऱ्या बोलिला ॥
जतन भाईनु करा । आमच्या संभाजीराजाला ॥
सराईत उमाजी राज्य (राजा) होईल तुम्हांला ॥
गड निरवितो गडकऱ्याला राज्य निरवितो नेतोजीला ॥
निरवानिरव दादानु । विनंती केली सकलीकाला ॥
"येथुनि सलाम सांगा । माझा शहाजी महाराजाला" ॥
खबर गेली जिजाऊला । शिवबा जातो भेटायला ॥
पालखींत बैसुनी । माता आली भेटायाला ॥२५॥

Verse 25 -He Shivaji Raje said to the killedars, "my Ram, Ram to you brothers take care of my Sambhaji Raje, the forts I submit to the care of the killedars, the Swarajya I submit to the care of Netoji Palkar, Give my respects to my Shahaji Maharaj."

Thus while he gave final instructions, the news reached Jijamata and she arrived in a palanquin.

चौक २६

शिवबा बोले जिजाऊ सवें । "बये वचन ऐकावें ॥
माझी आसोशी खानाला । "बये जातों भेटायाला" ॥
जिजाऊ बोले महाराजाला । "शिवबा न जावें भेटायाला ॥
मुसलमान बेइमान । खान राखिना तुम्हांला" ॥
राजा बोले जिजाऊला । "येवढी उंबर झाली भेट दिली नाहीं कोणाला ॥

येवढी गोष्ट माते । आज द्यावी मला ॥
आई अबदुलखान आला ॥ यानें धाक लाविला देवाला" ॥
जिजाऊ बोले महाराजाला । "शिवबा बुद्धिनें काम करावें ।
उसनें संभाजीचें घ्यावे" ॥२६॥

Verse 26- Shivaji Raje said to Jijamata "Khan is eager to meet me, so I must go, "Then Jijau said to Shivaji Raje". Shivba do not go to this meeting, this Muslim will not live to his promise. Khan has not come to protect you. Then Shivaji Raje said "Oh mother, in all my life I have never had such a meeting. So let me go for this meeting. Mother, Afzal Khan has destroyed the idols of Gods and Goddesses and by their blessings I alone can do this assignment. Then Jijamata gave this advice – use your intelligence to kill Afzal Khan. Take the revenge of the death of Sambhaji Raje (Shivaji Raje's elder brother killed at Kanakgiri)."

चौक २७

जिजाऊ घेती अलाबला । "शिवबा चढती दवलत तुला ॥
घे यशाचा विडा" । शिवबा स्मरे महादेवाला ।
गळां घातली मिठी । मातेच्या चरणासी लागला ॥
ध्यानीं आठवुनी भगवंताला । शिवाजी राजा सदरे गेला ॥२७॥

Verse 27- Jijamata then removed the ill effects of the evil eye on Shivaji Raje. And blessed him "Shivba your kingdom will increase day by day, so in this expedition you will return with success." Raje touched the feet of his mother and taking God's name he reached the shamiana.

चौक २८

"पहिला सलाम । माझा भवानीशंकराला ॥
दुसरा सलाम । माझा शहाजी महाराजाला ।
तिसरा सलाम । अमचे अबदुलखानाला " ।
शिवाजी सरजे सलाम केला । अबदुलखान (नानें) गुमान केला ॥

मनीं धरलें कपट । पुरतें कळलें महाराजाला ॥
मग तो शिवाजी सरज्याला । खान दापुनी बोलला ॥
"तूं तो कुणाबीका छोकरा । सवरत बाच्छाई सदरा" ॥२८॥

Verse 28- When he reached the shamiana, Raje made three salutations. The first salutation was to his family deity Tuljabhawani and Mahadev, the second to his father Shahaji Raje and the third to Afzal Khan. Seeing the lion like brave Shivaji Raje doing a salutation to him increased the arrogance in Afzal Khan. Shivaji Raje was aware of the treachery in Afzal Khan's mind. Khan said to Raje with contempt "you are a farmer's son yet you have furnished this shamiana like a Badshah."

चौक २९

इतक्या उपरी राजा बोले । त्या अबदुलखानाला ॥
"खाना ज्याची करणी त्याला । कांहीएक भ्यावें रघुनाथाला ॥
तुम्ही जातीचे कोण । आम्ही जाणतों तुम्हाला ॥
तूं तरी भटारनीका छोरा । शिवाजी सरज्यापर लाया तोरा" ॥
यावर अबदुल बोलला ॥ "शिवा तुम चलो विजापुराला" ॥
"शिवाजी सरजे नेतां । बहुत दिन लागतील खानाला ॥
कळला पुरुषार्थ । तुमचा बसल्या जाग्याला" ॥२९॥

Verse 29- On hearing this Raje said to Khan "One is known by one's work so you should be scared of Vishnu. I know which caste you belong to. You are the son of a cook and yet you lord over us." On this an enraged Afzal Khan said "Shiva you accompany me to Bijapur."

On this Raje said "Afzal Khan will require many days to take a lion like Shivaji Raje. It will not happen by giving orders whilst seated. Your bravery is now exposed."

चौक ३०

"अबदुल जातका भटारी । तुमने करना दुकानदारी" ॥
इतकिया उपरी । अबदुल मनीं खवळिला पुरा ॥
कव मारिलि अबदुल्याने । सरजा गवसून धरला सारा ॥
चालविली कटयार । सीलवर मारा न चाले जरा ॥
सराईत शिवाजी । त्यानें बिचव्याचा मारा केला ।
उजवे हातीं बिचवा त्याला । वाघनख सरजाच्या पंजाला ॥
उदरच फाडुनी । खानाची चरबी आणिली द्वारा ॥३०॥

Verse 30 - Raje taunted Khan "Afzal you are a cook by caste therefore, you should start an eatery (shop). On hearing this Khan lost his temper and became furious. Immediately Afzal squeezed Raje's (neck) in his armpit and struck him with a Katiyar. But Raje had worn an armor so that stab was ineffective. Raje dexterously used the tiger claws in his left hand to make a laceration, while with the bichhwa in his right hand he made incisive wound and pulled out his fat.

चौक ३१

खान "लव्हा लव्हा" बोलिला । खानाचा लव्हा बेगिन आला ॥
राजानें पट्टा पडताळिला । अबदुलखानानें हात मारिला ।
शिरींचा जिरेटोप तोडला । सरजा(ला) जरासा लागला ।
भला सराईत शिवाजी । पटयाचा गुंडाळा मारिला ॥
मान खांदा गवसुनी । जानव्याचा दोरा केला ॥
अबदुलखान शिवाजी दोनी । भांडती दोनी धुरा ॥
बारा हजार घोडा । सरदार नाहीं कोणी तिसरा ॥३१॥

Verse 31- Khan shouted "Dagga, Dagga." He was swiftly disemboweled. Raje took his dandpatta (long sword), but before that Afzal Khan made a stroke with his dagger, with so much force that Raje's headgear broke and it grazed his forehead causing a small wound. Raje struck a blow with his dandpatta such that it sliced Khan's neck and shoulder across (to the abdomen) like a janeu. (sacred thread) Thus both these warriors Afzal Khan and Shivaji Raje struck with their weapons and initiated the war. (Due to Raje's strategy) Khan's ....cavalry and his main sardars could not come to his aid.

चौक ३२

अबदुलखान झाला पुरा । कृष्णाजी ब्राह्मण उठावला ॥
शिवाजी राजा बोलला । "ब्राह्मणा मारुं नये तुला ।
तुजशीं मारतां शंकर हांसेल आम्हांला" ॥ नाइकतां ब्राह्मणें ।
हात दुसरा मारिला । "ब्राह्मणा मारुं नये तुला ।
क्रिया शहाजीची आम्हांला" ॥ कृष्णाजी ब्राह्मण(णें) ।
हात तिसरा टाकिला ॥ (तरी) होईल ब्रह्महत्या भोंसल्यासी ।
(म्हणून) शिवांजीनें राखिला ॥ कृष्णाजी ब्राह्मण मागें सरला ।
सैद बंडु मोहरे आला ॥ जवळ होता जिउ म्हाल्या ।
त्यानें सैद पुरा केला ॥३२॥

Verse 32-When Raje killed Afzal Khan Krishnaji Brahmin attacked Him with a weapon. Shivaji Raje said to him "If I kill a Brahmin Shrishankar (God) will ridicule me. So I shall not kill you." Krishnaji disregarded these words and struck at him a second time. Raje parried it saying, "Shahaji Raje has made us promise not to kill a Brahmin."Krishnaji struck a third time. Raje parried this attack also saying "The sin of killing a Brahmin should not rest on the Bhosle (family)." On hearing this Krishnaji retreated. Now Bada Sayyad charged on Shivaji Raje. But Jiwa Mahala who was near by killed him.

चौक ३३

संशय खानाचा फिटला । खान (नें) पळतां पाय काढिला ॥
मेळविला भोयांनीं । पालखींत घालून चालविला ॥
कावजीचा संभाजी भोंसला । मोठे उडीनें आला ॥

जखमा केल्या भोग्यांच्या पाया(ला) । खटारां धरणीवर पाडिला ।
शिवाजीराजा बेगिन आला । शिर कापुनी गडावर गेला ॥
जराचाच मंदिल । शिरीं त्या संभाजीचे घातला ॥
फाजिलखाना क्रोध आला । बाण आणि बंदुखा थोर वर्षाव एकच केला ॥
शिवाजीराजाचा चपाटा । फाजिलखान बारा वाटा ॥
हाल महाराजाचे झाले । अबदूलच्या लोकांला ॥३३॥

Verse 33- In this confusion Afzal Khan tried to slip out of the shamiana and came to his palanquin. The bearers put him in the palanquin and ran towards his camp. Sambhaji Kavji ran fast and cut off the legs of the bearers, (bringing) the palanquin crashing down. By this time, Raje reached there and they cut off the head of the Khan and went to the Pratapgad. Raje was pleased by his bravery and (therefore) placed a head gear on his head.

When (Afzal Khan's son) Fazal Khan came to know of his death he became very angry and started shooting arrows and bullets. But under the assault by Shivaji Raje, Fazal Khan's army started dispersing in all twelve directions.

चौक ३४

प्रतापगडाहुनि केला हल्ला । मारिती खुण सरज्याच्या लोकांला ॥
धरल्या चारी वाटा । ज्यांनीं घाट बळकाविला ॥
दळ त्या समई । पायदळाचा कडका आला ॥
सिलीमकर, खोपडया, । काकडया, सुरव्या, लोटला ॥
अंगद हनुमंत रघुनाथाला । पायचे पायदळ शिवाजीराजाला ॥
"फिरंग ठेवी जाउद्या, त्याला । राखु नका तुम्ही उगारल्या पाइकाला" ॥
फत्ते महाराजाची झाली । वाट दिली कुलवजीराला ॥३४॥

Verse 34-After the clash at Pratapgad the people of the lion hearted (king) closed all the exit routes from Jawli and pounced on the Khan's army. The Maratha infantry which had closed the all the trails to the mountain top now assaulted the Khan's army. Just as Angad and Hanuman was to Ram, so also Raje's sardars Shilimkar, Khopde, Kakde Suryarao overwhelmed Khan's army. "Maharaj gave strict orders : he who puts down his weapon and surrenders may be spared but, he who raises his weapon, kill him without mercy."Accordingly those sardar of the Khan who relented were set free.

चौक ३५
पळतां फाजिलखान । त्याचा दुमाळा घेतला ॥
माघारा फिरोनि । जान(नें) हातीचा आरोबा दिला ॥
शिवाजीचे हाल । फाजिलखान घाय (यें) पुरा केलाअ ।
घोडा आणि राऊत । ज्यांणीं पाडाव केला ॥
वळल्या हातीवरल्या ढाला । चार हजार घोडा अबदुल्या जावळींत बुडविला ॥
भवानी शंकर प्रसन्न ज्याला । यश राज्याला खंडयाला ।
सरज्या तोरड महीमोर्तब शिवाजीला । फत्ते झाली महाराजाची ते वेळ पन्हाळा घेतला
॥३५॥

Verse 35 -During this turmoil, the immensely injured Fazal Khan left behind his horses and army and escaped from Jawli. These were gathered by Raje's army. The Adilshahi flags on the elephants were discarded and they were merged in the Maratha army. Shivaji Raje and Marathas gathered the complete army of Afzal Khan in Jawli. This campaign was successful because of Dev Mahadev and Tuljabhawani were pleased with Raje's sword (bravery). Raje collected all the Khan's battle standards (flags). Immediately after this grand achievement, Maharaj took the Adilshahi fort of Panhalgad.

चौक ३६
अज्ञानदास विनवी श्रोत्याला । राजा अवतारी जन्मला ॥
नळनीळ सुग्रीव जांबूवंत । अंगद हनुमंत रघुनाथाला ॥
एकांती भांडन । जैसें राम रावणाला ॥
तैसा शिवाजी सरजा । एकांती नाटोपे कवणाला ॥

दृष्टी पर्यस शिवाजीला । कलीमधीं अवतार जन्मला ॥
विश्वाची जननी । अंबा बोले शिवाजीला ॥
मोठें भक्तीचें फळ । महादेव भाकेला गोंविला ॥
जिकडे जाती, तिकडे यश राज्याच्या खंडाला ॥३६॥

Verse 36- The Shahir (bard /poet) Adyandas says that , this king is "a manifestation of God created to release the earth from the clutches of the Muslims." Just as in the army of Prabhu Ramchandra though there were many brave warriors like Nal-Neel, Sugriv, Jambuvant, Angad, Hanumant etc. but to assassinate Ravan, Prabhu Ramchandra had to himself fight similarly when the lion like brave Shivaji Raje entered the battle field no one could defeat him. Shivaji Raje was a reincarnation of God in this Kaliyug. The Mother of the Universe Jagdamba and Mahadev (Shiva) were pleased with Shivaji Raje and gave fructation to his worship (by aiding in the elimination of Afzal Khan). Thence the swords of Swarajya were victorious in all directions.

चौक ३७

माता जिजाऊ बोलली । पोटीं अवतार जन्मला ॥
शंकपाळ शिवाजी महाराजानें केला । आतां मी गाईन ।
भोंसले शिवरायाच्या ख्याति ॥ दावा हेवा जाण ।
अखेर संग्रामाच्या गति ॥ राजगड राजाला ।
प्रतापगड जिजाऊला ॥ धन्य जिजाऊचे कुशी ।
राजा अवतार जन्मला ॥ आपल्या मतें अज्ञानदासानें ।
बीरमाल राज्याचा गाइला ॥ शिवाजी सरज्यानें ।
इनाम घोडा बक्षीस दिला ॥ शेरभर सोन्याचा ।
तोडा हातांत घातला ॥ यश जगदंबेचें ।
तुळजा प्रसन्न शिवराजाला ॥३७॥

Verse 37 – A joyous Mata Jijau said, "Raje was a reincarnation who was born in her womb." The Shahir (bard) Adnyandas sings the praises of Shivraya of the Bhosle family. After this terrible war there was no loss to Swarajya as all the forts remained with Shivaji Raje. (infact all the Adilshahi area up to Kolhapur -Panhalgad was conquered)

(I)Adyandas with my limited intelligence have tried to describe the bravery of Raje. (On hearing it) the lion hearted courageous king presented him with a bracelet weighing one seer and a horse. Jagadamba and (family Goddess) Tulzabhawani was pleased it was due her blessings that Raje was triumphant.

CHRONOLOGY

1594	- Birth of Shahaji Raje
1598	- Birth of Jijamata
1610	- Shahaji Raje marries Jijabai
1629	- July 25: Murder of Lakhoji Jadhav at Nizamshahi Dabar
1630	- Feb 19: Birth of Shivaji Raje
1637	- Adil Shah grants Pune Jagir to Shahaji Raje
1640	- Shivaji Raje visits Shahaji Raje at Banglore
1646-1656	- Illness and death of Mohamed Adilshah
1646	- Shivaji Raje gains Torna
1647	- Shivaji Raje gains Kondana
1648	- July 25: Shahaji Raje arrested by Adilshah at Jinji
1648	- October 09: Shivaji Raje takes Fort Purandar
1656	- Jan 15: Shivaji Raje gains Jawli
1656	- Apr 06: Shivaji Raje gains Rairi
	- Aug 28: Baji Chandrarao More escapes to Bijapur
	- Aurangzeb's second viceroyalty of Deccan
1657	- Aurangzeb's Invasion Of Bijapur
	- Shivaji Raje writes to Aurangzeb
	- 23 Apr: Aurangzeb writes to Shivaji Raje
	- 27 Apr: Battle of Kalyani -Bidar
	- 30 Apr: Shivaji Raje attacks Junner
	- 14 May: Birth of Sambhaji
	- 24 Oct: Shivaji Raje Kalian Bhivandi
1658	- 08 Jan: Shivaji Raje takes Mahuli
	- 08 Jan: Shivaji Raje at Rajgad
	- 20 Mar: Aurangzeb starts from Burhanpur for Agra

	- 21 July: First Enthronement of Aurangzeb
	- 30 July: Shivaji Raje sends Sonopant to Delhi
	- Shahaji denies responsibility for Shivaji Raje's action
1659	- Afzal Khan was appointed to take on Shivaji Maharaj
	- April: Adil Shah orders Mawal deshmukhs to join Afzal Khan
	- July 11: Shivaji Raje goes to Jawli
	- Sep 05: Saibai dies
	- Oct: Kanhoji Jedhe and other Deshmukhs decide to stand by Shivaji Raje
	- Krishnaji Bhaskar meets Shivaji Raje
	- Nov 10: Elimination of Afzal Khan
	- Nov 11: The Marathas reach Wai
	- Nov 28: Panhalgad captured
	- Dec 28: Rustam e Jaman defeated near Kolhapur
1660	- Jan: Netoji Palkar sent to capture Adilshahi
	- Jan to March: Shivaji Raje lays siege to Miraj
	- March 2: Siddi Jauhar starts from Kunoor for Miraj
	- Shivaji Raje takes refuge in Panhalgad
	- Shaista Khan reaches Maharashtra
	- Mar to July: Shivaji Raje trapped in Panhalgad
	- July 1-3: Shivaji Raje gives charge of Panhalgad to Trimbak Bhaskar and escapes from Panhalgad
	- July 13: Death of Shiva Kashid
	- July 14: Death of Baji Prabhu at Pawan Khind
	- August: Khandoji Khopde made chaurang
	- August: Shaisa Khan takes Chakan from Murar Baji
	- Sep 22: Treaty with Adil Shah. Panhalgad surrendered
1661	- Jan 20: Battle of Umer Khind (Kartalab Khan)

	- March: Attack on Rajapur. Revington imprisoned.
1663	- April 06: Strike on Shaista Khan

REFERENCES

English

BI - Bijapur Inscriptions/Dr M Nazim

C S - Chhatrapati Shivaji / Setu Madhavrao Pagdi

CSSHI - Chhatrapati Shivaji: Savior of Hindu India / G B Mehendale

GW 1 - Guerrilla Warfare /Mao Tse Tung

GW 2 - Guerrilla Warfare /Walter Laqueur

ERS - English Records on Shivaji

HOA - History of Aurangzeb V1-5/Sir Jadunath Sarkar

HOS - House of Shivaji

HMI - History of Mughal India/V D Mahajan

MA/ Sir Jadunath Sarkar

MIA - Masir I Alamgiri /Saki Mustad Khan

MI - Medieval India

MLL - Muntakhabu-L-Lubab/Muhammad Hashim, Khafi Khan

NCHI - The New Cambridge History Of India: Vol 1

PMR - Portuguese Mahratta Relations/ Pissulenkar-TR Parvate

RIAEH - Rulers of India: Aurangzeb, Emperor of Hindusthan/ Lan

SHA - Short History of Aurangzeb /Sir Jadunath sarkar

SCSAB - Shiv Chhatrapati (Sabhasad)/ Surendranath Sen

SHT - Shivaji and His Times/Jadunath Sarkar

STGM - Shivaji the Great Maratha /H S Sardesai

SHLT - Shivaji His Life and Times /G B Mehendale

SAR - Studies in Aurangzeb's Reign /Jadunath Sarkar

TRME - Travels in the Mughal Empire/Francis Bernier

LSM - The Life of Shivaji Maharaj /N S Takakhav

TME - The Mughal Empire /Ashirbadilal Shrivastava

Marathi

१. रायगडची जीवनकथा/ शांताराम विष्णू आवळसकर

२. छत्रपती शिवाजीमहाराज/ कृष्णराव अर्जुन केळूसकर

३. शककर्ते शिवराय/ शिवकथाकार विजयराव देशमुख

४. शिवाजी कोण होता? / गोविंद पानसरे

५. श्री छत्रपति शिवाजी महाराज/ श्री वा. सी. बेंद्रे

६. शिवछत्रपतींचे आरमार/ ग. भा. मेहंदळे व सं. प्र. शिंत्रे

७. छत्रपती शिवाजी महाराजांची राजधर्मसूत्रे/ मोहिनी दातार

८. शिवकालातील दुर्ग व दुर्गव्यवस्था/ महेश तेंडुलकर

९. अथतो दुर्गजिज्ञासा/ प्र. के. घाणेकर

१०. शिवकाल १६३० ते १७०७ इ. / डॉ. वि. गो. खोबरेकर

१२. शिवछत्रपती: एक मागोवा/ डॉ. जयसिंगराव पवार

१३. औरंगजेबाचा इतिहास/ सर जदुनाथ सरकार/ भाषांतरकार डॉ. भ. गा. कुंटे

१४. छत्रपती शिवाजी/ सेतूमाधवराव पगडी

१५. शिवचरित्रापासून आम्ही काय शिकावे/ डॉ. जयसिंगराव पवार

१६. मध्ययुगीन भारताचा बृहत इतिहास/ जे. एल. मेहता/ भाषांतर डॉ. वसंतराव देशपांडे

१७. पुण्यश्लोक छत्रपती शिवाजी/ साहित्याचार्य बाळशास्त्री हरदास

१९. मराठा रियासत शककर्ता शिवाजी/ गो. स. सरदेसाई

२०. श्री शिवछत्रपती: संकल्पित शिवचरित्राची प्रस्तावना, आराखडा व साधने/ त्र्यंबक शंकर शेजवलकर

२१. श्री शिवभारत/ सदाशिव महादेव दिवेकर

२२. मराठ्यांचा इतिहास/ अ. रा. कुलकर्णी आणि ग. ह. खरे

२३. प्रतापगडचे युद्ध/ कॅप्टन गणेश मोडक

२४. राजा शिवछत्रपती/ बाबासाहेब पुरंदरे

Dr Hemant Raje Gaikwad

Dr. Hemant Raje Gaikwad did his MBBS DOMS from Grant Medical College where he was the General Secretary of the Students Union.

In 1999 to celebrate the silver jubilee of his batch he wrote this breezy book on his college days named. 'Chakaraka Makaraka' The book is now in forth print.

As a student (1974-80) he was awarded.

1) The Rao Bahadur Maniar award for skin and veneral disease.

2) The B. B. Yodh research fellowship.

3) The prize paper at Bombay Medi Meet.

He has won many prizes in debating, rock-climbing and badminton at the College / University Competitions.

In 1980 during his internship he founded the Chirner rural medical centre which grew into a forty bed rural hospital. He was presented the **Rajiv Gandhi Shiromani** by joint committee of Governors for the same.

He has conducted many medical camps and was commended by the then **Speaker of India, Shri Manohar Joshi**.

He had a strong desire to serve the nation and to fulfill his love for the uniform in 1986 he joined the Home Guards as medical officer and he rose to be the **Commandant of Greater Mumbai.**

He was commended by the then **Lieutenant Governor of Andaman and Nicobar, Shri Ram Kapse** for his activity during the Tsunami.

During his tenure he started the **Railway Suraksha Pathak** to prevent harassment / molestation of lady commuters. Today the duties also encompass the checking of commuters for concealed bombs.

He is recipient of **two service medals.**

1) **Swatantrata Suvarna Jayanti Padak - 1997.**

2) **Maharashtra Rajya Home Guard Hirak Jayanti Padak - 2006.**

He also specifically enrolled fishermen as Home Guards to guard the coast line of Mumbai especially important after the **26 / 11 / 2008** terrorist attack on Mumbai city.

He was also instrumental in organizing the first three **Mumbai Marathons.**

He has also been commended by **WHO for Pulse Polio**

He is the director of the Dr. Gaikwad Institute which has trained more than 7000 paramedics in the last **twenty-five years**. Dr. Gaikwad was the Regional officer (Maharashtra) for Bharat Sevak Samaj whose founder president was Pt Jawaharlal Nehru. BSS was previously 'The Servant of India Society' founded by Shri Gopal Khrishna Gokhale in 1902.

He was presented the **Outstanding Principal Award by Lions Clubs International**. He is also recipient of Bharatiya Chikitsa Ratna Award.

He has written twenty **manuals for nursing homes**.

His short stories / articles have appeared in Midday, Free Press, Indian Express, Times Of India, Debonair, PEN (India).

He has been awarded **The Economic Times - Icon Of Excellence Award And Bharat Karmasri Award By Central Bharat Sewak Samaj.**

His aim in life is " to give Chhatrapati Shivaji Maharaj his due status in World History."

His book **'Shivaji Maharaj the Greatest'** (Marathi) has became a best seller and has been awarded the Granthalaya Bharati S G Kashikar Award. It is now in fourth edition and translated in Hindi, English and will soon be translated in Sanskrit, Kannada and Bangla.

It has been made into a documentary film in Marathi, Hindi, English, Kannada & Sanskrit. The film has won awards by.

1) Mumbai University (Kannada Dept.).

2) Shivaji Mandir, Dadar. Mumbai.

3) Sanskrit Bharati, Nashik.

4) Sayadri Pratisthan , Pune.

5) Mumbai Pradesh Congress Committee, Mumbai.

6) Shri Shivrajyabhishek Dinotsav Seva Samitee, Durgraj, Raigad.

His family consists of wife Dr. Pushpa who is an Ophthalmic Surgeon, son Dr. Gaurang a Homeopath and daughter Dr. Gunjan a Dental Surgeon who is married to Shri. Harshal. Dr Hemant is blessed with a grandson Hriday.

He can be contacted on 9870535310 / 8691840551

Or gaikwadhemant510@gmail.com

www.ingramcontent.com/pod-product-compliance
Lightning Source LLC
LaVergne TN
LVHW061610070526
838199LV00078B/7232